Come Back Frayed

COLIN WRIGHT

Asymmetrical Press
Missoula, Montana

Published by Asymmetrical Press
Missoula, Montana.

Library of Congress Cataloging-In-Publication Data
Come Back Frayed / Colin Wright — 1st ed.
ISBN: 978-1-68287-003-7
eISBN: 978-1-68287-002-0
WC: 56,668
1. Memoir. 2. Travel. 3. Tales. 4. Philosophy.
5. Lifestyle.

Cover design by Colin Wright
Formatted in beautiful Montana
Printed in the U.S.A.

Publisher info:
Website: www.asymmetrical.co
Email: howdy@asymmetrical.co
Twitter: @asympress

ASYM METR ICAL

ACKNOWLEDGEMENTS

A great big thanks to the folks who helped me whip this book into suitable shape for publication:

Matt Doyle, Robert Witham, Türkan Atlam, Yitzchak Young, and Shawn Mihalik.

Any typos or other mistakes are probably the result of me ignoring their damn good advice.

For the people of Mayoyao and the storms of Boracay.

Clouds come floating into my life, no longer to carry rain or usher storm, but to add color to my sunset sky.

—RABINDRANATH TAGORE

There are no foreign lands. It is the traveler only who is foreign.

—ROBERT LOUIS STEVENSON

Come Back Frayed

BEFORE

INTRO

I make more sense in motion.

There's a storm just outside my door as I write this. I'm on a small island in the Philippines, and there's a typhoon up north, carving into the shores of the larger island where I was living a few weeks ago. We're only seeing wisps of the tail here, backwash from the core action, but it's enough to shake up the atmosphere, the air vibrating with adjacent activity. The beach is vacant except for a few brazen locals and ignorant visitors, pushing themselves into the waves and walking the beaches, leaning into the stinging force of the wind, hoping that their frantic fun won't take a turn, praying that they don't become a statistic, a tale told to forewarn children of the dangers inherent to island living. Ghost stories for resort-dwellers.

I'm one of these people, one of these potential projectiles. I've spent the day wind-whipped, coming up with excuses to leave the little studio apartment I've rented a few steps from the beach, watching as the surf climbs upward, first beyond the usual tide-line, then beyond the flag that displays the direction and freneticness of the wind, its rip-stop fabric torn in places, its outline a blur as it's tugged by the 60 mph winds and 80 mph gusts. The water is creeping toward the chairs that are replaced each morning by restaurant owners, which on a normal day provide spots where tourists can sit with drinks and international foods while ogling the ocean from what's typically a safe distance. That perception of safety is fading: the giant umbrellas were removed yesterday, and the chairs are being eyeballed by managers, each wondering if they can wait out the worst of the wind or if they'll have to whip-crack their underlings into chair-moving action from the loll they've fallen into during this lull.

I'm two coffees into my day, each acquired from a different location and each representing one less legitimate excuse to step out into the elemental fray. The weather has been swelteringly hot, shirt-drenchingly humid, for weeks. There's still a stickiness to the air, but the temperature has plummeted. It's 85 degrees Fahrenheit today, but it feels like 75. The gale chaps my skin and cools my permanent glaze of sweat, transforming the moisture-heavy air into something not just tolerable, but pleasant. The feel of the wind in my hair, on my face, across my bare legs and arms, is marvelous. I can't get enough of it. After two weeks of sweating out every drop of water I've ever consumed, all day, every day, the relief is like the deep, complete exhale of a long-held breath. The predictability of postcard-worthy beach weather wears at me, and this island is ensconced by the same class of climate that fed my discontent with Los Angeles many years ago. I crave randomness. An ever-present environmental element that I can't control. I need to wake up and not know what to expect so that I can go out and pursue the unexpected.

I've had relationships in which my partner has said they

didn't really know me until we traveled together. It's not that I'd ever held anything back, they said, or that I was different in any quantifiable way while wandering. But aspects of my character, my habits, even things like my haircut and facial expressions and category of confidence didn't fully make sense to them until we were in transit. Once on the road, though, it all fit.

We're shaped by our environments, just as we shape the places in which we live. Humans are skilled at stomping around and inventing solutions to problems and turning things into other things, but as we alter the world, so too are we altered. Our habits and our outlooks and even our genes, all in flux. Our habits become traditions, our outlooks become focused perspectives, and we become people who are partially defined by our habitats. Our homes.

A person without a home, or as I prefer to think of it, a person with many homes, is defined in part by that lifestyle. Shaped by mobility and a lack of permanent roots. Such a person must bend, lest they break. Must get along in order to get along. Must roll with the punches by default.

My clothing is durable and modular: everything goes with everything else. My work is an assemblage of projects I can do from anywhere and is burdened with few infrastructural necessities. My relationships are in large part shaped by where I am at the moment, and the deep, lasting partnerships are the kind that transcend physical location. My workout and hygiene regimens are routines that I can perform predictably so long as I have a prison cell-sized area in which to move. I've adopted a hair style that can grow long and heavily disarrayed while still appearing somewhat intentional.

I enjoy holding still sometimes, slowing down and taking stock. Assessing and processing. But the moment I get back out there, the moment I arrive at an airport or a train station, or board a bus, or hop on a boat, or start walking a path that will take me someplace new, I can feel the difference. I feel like I've arrived. Like I'm back in a place where I can be truly and completely myself again. I don't have to realign and reshape, or convince myself that I entirely enjoy having everything neat and tidy and controlled.

I no longer need to tolerate the weather being the same every day.

Should the wind or rain become typhonic, should the ocean move uncomfortably far inland, should plans fall apart and the unexpected become the norm, should the world suddenly spin wildly and thrust me into something for which I'm not prepared, while I'm out here on the road, at least, I'm not expected to step back and go inside and wait for it all to pass. I can walk in that wind, I can get ruffled and wet and worn. I can use and abuse my possessions because that's what they're for: to get me where I want to go, wherever that happens to be, whether or not there's an existing path that will guide me there.

I make more sense in motion. While moving, experiencing new things, feeling a little uncomfortable and always somewhat off-balance, while pursuing new ways of looking at life, at people, at society — that's when the world makes the most sense to me.

EXPERIMENT

My life is optimized for opportunity.

None of us can control everything that happens to and around us, and that's accurate to the umpteenth for those who travel. The best you can hope for is a little deck-stacking here and there, and a carefully sharpened ability to play whatever cards you're dealt. Sometimes that means folding, stepping away from the table, and playing another game for a while. Sometimes it means you're handed some dice instead, or a random handful of obscure game paraphernalia with purposes you haven't yet discovered. In such cases all you can do is plaster a confident expression across your face, watch those around you for clues, and hope to hell you figure out the rules before it's your turn to play.

I started traveling full-time nearly seven years ago, and in that time I've learned many new sets of rules, many new ways to play innumerable different games. I trial-and-errored my way into the publishing industry, segueing from brand-work and a harried lifestyle of entrepreneurship into something like that classic caricature of an author: I fixate on my work, sometimes sequestering myself from all else so that I might better obsess over assembling sentences with closer-to-ideal compositions for the stories I want to tell.

The catalyst behind many of my experiments has been the desire to maintain balance in my lifestyle. I'm not wealthy, but I make enough to pay the bills, and I'm hungry to learn and create. To engage in rampant intellectual consumption and production.

How might I perpetuate this lifestyle in a healthy way? How might I sustain this rhythm that has allowed me to hurl myself nose-first at creative fulfillment while still pursuing new adventures, new creative and entrepreneurial pursuits, and new opportunities?

Also: how far can I push before experiencing an untenable extreme?

I gave my first professional, public talk in front of an audience about six years ago, speaking at a New Zealand university to a crowd of design and illustration students.

I sucked. It was bad. The story was compelling to some, but my presentation was unpracticed, unwieldy. Embarrassing. As someone who was transitioning into professional authorship and telling stories for a living, it wasn't my finest moment.

But it did help me recognize that storytelling, regardless of the delivery medium utilized, is still storytelling. There were many people I could reach through my blog, through my books, through my tweets and social media posts, but there were just as many who didn't read books and didn't spend their time online. I would have to speak to these people in a different way if I wanted to interact with them.

Typically, the medium is less important than the message.

That's not to say that the medium is trivial. On the contrary, just as musicians have had their craft shaped, first by the spaces in which they performed, then by the vinyl upon which their music was etched, then by the magnetic tape woven through a plastic cassette cartridge, then by the laser spirals on a compact disc, and today by the bitrates and file sizes which determine the ease of online streaming, so too are authors influenced by distribution channels, the prices and availability of printing ink, paper thicknesses, and increasingly, the prevalence of ebook readers and smartphones. The size and clarity of those screens and the battery life that powers them determines how people consume your ideas and whether or not they'll see them in the first place.

I've become vehicle agnostic. I care less about how I reach people and more about reaching them in the first place.

There was a time when I would have hesitated before stepping foot in front of a crowd. There was a time when people who watched videos online were a mystery to me, and I was content to write words I hoped to someday convince someone to read. There was a time when I felt my writing, vocabulary encoded with twenty-six bit alphabetic iconography, was the sole practical and relevant mechanism I had of presenting and exchanging ideas with others.

Today, I'm of the opinion that if you want to reach someone, to really communicate in a language they understand and trust, you have to be more flexible. Like an illustrator who's only ever worked with graphite but who's learning how to oil paint, I'm finding that the ability to tell stories, to communicate ideas, to interact with someone else intellectually is not a finite skill limited by the tools I've used in the past. Drawing is not the same as painting, but there are sufficient similarities that an illustrator has a leg-up when learning how to apply the right brush strokes, how to mix colors, and how to treat a canvas.

I've been an illustrator, I've been a designer, I've been an author and a blogger. Why not a public speaker? Why not a producer? Why not a podcaster or narrator or TV show host or video game developer?

Why should we limit ourselves to what we already know, particularly when what we've experienced can help us transition to other paths, help us achieve other skill sets, help us pursue new opportunities?

Extremes are insidious because they're incredibly valuable until they're not. At some point on the usefulness curve, they transition, Hyde-like, to harmful. Even water is deadly if you drink too much of it.

Avoiding extremes has become an integral part of my lifestyle, because I find that walking up to that line, toeing it, and then stepping back to stand on healthier, more stable ground is what allows me to work and live and enjoy the world around me without suffering the consequences of burnout, sleep-deprivation, ill-health, and fanaticism.

Frustratingly, one can even become too extreme about avoiding extremes: I try to weave them into my lifestyle periodically to ensure that I'm not missing out on something wonderful just on the other side of that line.

What's treacherous about extremes is that it can be difficult to recognize when you're neck-deep in one. Something that may have at one point seemed logical, rational, and well thought out can over time creep upward, wax and expand, until suddenly your coffee habit has become something else entirely: a coffee addiction, a reliance on that caffeine-bean, a drink that's become a necessary component to your day, and one that, when absent, punches a mug-shaped hole in your life.

It's possible to enjoy a thing, to even habitualize a thing, without it becoming a troublesome burden. The trick is to test your relationship with it from time to time, openly explore alternatives, consider that your habit might be negative for you in some way, and assess your escape routes should that prove to be the case.

This is something I do with coffee. One out of every four months is a coffee-free month, for me. If I come back to it on the fifth, as I always have so far, I can return it to my life with more enthusiasm than ever because I know for a fact that it's still a positive addition to my day. And I can more confidently trust that judgement because it's made while outside the influence of the habit in question. Enjoyment without reliance is one of the purest, healthiest forms of pleasure.

I realized a year ago that there was a facet of my life with which I hadn't experimented in some time. From when I first started traveling full-time, the framework guiding my lifestyle has included four month stints in one country before moving to another, each location voted upon by my readers. This methodology had continued more or less unchanged since I started using it back in 2009.

I wondered whether it might be time to poke at that clay and see if it had become brittle. If perhaps it was time to re-wet the surface, make it malleable again. I wanted to assure myself that this structure was something I could continue to shape as my needs and wants evolved, rather than becoming an unthinking habit that requires I shape myself to it.

An opportunity emerged. I'd spent a few months reading and writing and whittling away at my workload from a basement in the Midwest. I had set aside the time to recover from a book tour that had been both wildly successful and a significant energy drain, and I was aching to get back out into the world, to experience something new once more. I tallied the votes my readers had cast during the preceding months and the numbers declared that my next home country would be the Philippines.

While planning the announcement of my next destination, however, I booked two speaking gigs: one for a Writer's Guild event in Columbia, Missouri, and one for a social media conference in Bogotá, Colombia. These events would take place less than a week apart. If I left for the Philippines soon, I could stay in the country for two months before hustling back to the Americas for my speaking engagements. Rather than staying in one city for four months as usual, I decided to try living in two different places within the Philippines, each for one month. I could compare and contrast those experiences, achieving a breadth of cultural experience rather than my usual focused depth.

The Philippines being an island nation, it seemed like a good place to try this remix of my usual method. Cultures have a greater opportunity to fragment and diversify when casual inter-city travel is impeded by the landscape.

I use AirBnB frequently while on the road in the US, but hadn't yet used it elsewhere in the world. Because I'd have less time to hunt for an apartment in the Philippines, I decided to peruse the AirBnB network for a pair of month-long homes in two different Filipino cities. The rentals I found were better than I could have hoped for.

Opportunities. They abound when you open yourself up to them, calibrate for non-rigidity, and push back against internal extremism, allowing yourself and your lifestyle to be well-rounded and healthy.

From there, you just have to go and do.

SPEAK ATTEND ARRIVE

For nearly two months, I hermited.

Post-book-tour, post-being-social nearly all day for weeks on end, I visited my parents, the dual-purpose of the visit being the opportunity to catch up with my family while also hiding out and working on all the things I'd put off leading up to my social downswing.

Columbia, Missouri is a wonderful place for this because there's very little 'fear of missing out.' I can retreat to LA or NY to hermit, but there are always countless social engagements I want to attend, and that magnetism pulls me from my isolated, creative reverie. CoMo, on the other hand, has things going on, but not an over-abundance of things. I can grind on a project for days without needing to come up for air, focusing on eating well, working out, writing and writing and writing, recording my thoughts and stories in the cavernous inner rooms of the now-mostly-empty ranch-style where I spent most of my childhood, looking inward rather than outward for a time. A true privilege, if you can carve out the space for it.

This particular batch of Midwest-based isolation was also the build up toward a week of unfamiliarity and extroversion. I bounced to Denver, where I attended a conference called the Colorado Innovation Network Summit. I had been invited to give a talk to attendees on the topic of minimalism, and though I'm not certain I was the youngest person there, the demographic was certainly skewed upward. I was introduced by the Governor of Colorado as 'a Millennial,' which was a first for me, but also an indicator of the average age of those attending.

I truly enjoy sharing ideas I care about with audiences of all compositions, and it's particularly thrilling to be the first to introduce a concept, cohesively, to someone.

While up on stage in Denver, the acoustics were such that I couldn't tell if the crowd was engaged or asleep, so their response to my words could have leaned toward either enthusiasm or ennui. This was a group of businesspeople, government higher-ups, and nonprofit organizers, and there's always the chance that the concept of simplifying, reducing clutter, and slicing away unnecessary bureaucracy will land with a resounding thud.

Though visually unresponsive from my spot on stage, attendees were actually very much into the idea. I had trouble doing much of anything post-talk for both days of the conference, as attendees and other speakers engaged me to express their thanks and congratulations on the presentation. It's a blast speaking about things I care about to anyone, but it's especially gratifying when people who're not part of your typical audience respond so positively.

The conference only lasted two days, but it shattered my sleep schedule. I'd enjoyed months of a luxurious 'waking whenever' lifestyle, and in Denver I bolted awake to the sound of my early-set alarm both days, then once more each for my flights in and out of Colorado. I was also socially 'on' the entire time I was at the summit, which, my being a half-and-half introvert-extrovert — a well-balanced ambivert, I like to think — wore me out.

I flew back to Missouri for a day to sleep a little and grab the other half of my possessions before flying to the coast. Los Angeles was supposed to be a quiet little stop on the way to something brand new. A brief, uneventful little layover during which I'd eat some Mexican food (as one must do in LA), beeline for my rented bed for some anticipatory sleep, then pop back to the airport for my flight to the Philippines.

This did not happen.

A few weeks before the trip my good friend and amazing person Felicia invited me to be her date for the MTV Video Music Awards. The show took place on the one full day I'd be in the city.

There was a moment when I thought, "No Colin. Remember sleep? You should sleep that day." But that moment passed. I have a policy when traveling that, in general, I should say 'Yes' far more than 'No,' the latter only in circumstances where 1. saying 'yes' would mean certain death, or 2. I'm actually worn out to the point of being sick. Neither was likely to be the case, so I accepted the invitation and began working the VMAs into my schedule.

This didn't require much adjustment, calendar-wise. I already had my plane tickets, and the timing wasn't too obtrusive. I would need something more blingy to wear, because I'm seldom blingy, so I designed a shirt with a quote from one of my books, the lettering in gold vinyl. The shirt read: "Every second is a finite resource you can spend on everything or nothing." I also packed my suit jacket, which I planned to leave, along with the shirt, with Felicia before leaving Los Angeles. I didn't think I'd get much mileage out of either while in the Philippines.

Since my original plan for a passive LA visit was botched, I doubled-down on making the most of my time there. I reached out to a few friends I hadn't seen in ages and managed to set up a rough schedule that would allow me to visit with several of them on the day I arrived.

After the flight touched down in LAX, I met up with my ex-girlfriend, current-very-good-friend Andi, a gal with whom I'd lived when I was an LA resident nearly seven years ago. I then met up with my friend Lisa, a producer who I hadn't seen in ages, and with whom there was some TV-related business to discuss. Next was a coffee and catch-up with someone I'd dated while living in Prague who was in LA visiting her boyfriend. Afterward, I connected with Felicia and our VMA double-date couple for fancy Mexican food.

Thankfully, we all managed to get a little sleep before the hectic next day.

The VMA event began in the afternoon, and its after-parties continued deep into the evening. I had a ticket for a redeye from LAX to Tokyo that same day, my flight leaving at 1am, so I would miss the parties and much of the associated debauchery. I like to arrive at the airport early for international flights in case something is wrong with the booking or on the off-chance there's a visa issue that needs to be handled before I can board. As such, I left shortly after the televised portion of the award show.

The event itself was interesting. I use that word because I'm not really a part of MTV's demographic, so I didn't really know who any of the celebrities were, and as someone who's worked in branding I can't help but see such shows as a brand-building exercise rather than as pure entertainment. But viewing anything through an anthropological lens can make it interesting, and it certainly was that. I was also in good company, and when the show was over I regretted having to leave so early for the airport. We all hustled back to our rented townhouse and I changed out of my bling-shirt, dialed up an Uber, and was on my way to LAX.

I prefer long flights or very short ones. Flights of middling duration are the worst. A flight of fifty minutes isn't bad, and a flight of twelve hours is great, because for the former you've arrived after reading a chapter of a book, and for the latter you can safely sleep, deeply engage with a book, watch a bunch of movies, write like crazy, or whatever else catches your fancy. The tedious flights, to me, are the ones that last maybe two to five hours, a period that is not short enough for you to get through casually, and not long enough for you to entrench and mentally commit to sitting still for a while.

My flight to Tokyo took about ten hours, during which I slept a solid six. I cannot overstate how wonderful this was. I do sleep on long-haul flights, but typically in twenty minute stints. These add up once you've had enough of them, but don't quite give you that well-rested feeling when you touch down. When I arrived in Tokyo, though, I felt great, upbeat even. I strolled around the not-quite-awake airport, enjoying the optimistic vision of a pleasant, robo-centric future-from-the-'90s that a lot of Japanese buildings seem to exude. I snagged a coffee and croissant, but only to tide me over until the curry place in the food court opened a few hours later. There was a Japanese curry restaurant across the street from where I stayed during my final week living in Bangkok, and I got hooked on the dish. It's comfort food, and occupies a cultural space similar to that of mac n' cheese in the US.

Post-curry, I boarded my shorter, five-hour flight to Manila. The journey wasn't horrible, but also wasn't as pleasant as the lengthier leg to Japan. I read and read and read, churning through the last few dozen pages of *Infinite Jest* and knocking out *Starship Troopers* (which I hadn't read in over ten years) in its entirety.

When I landed, I had two main objectives: to acquire a SIM card for my phone, and to extend my visa from the default month to double that. Both objectives needed to be completed before the next morning when I would begin my overland journey to a remote mountain town called Mayoyao, where I would spend my first month in the country.

I arrived in the early afternoon, Manila-time, but as it turned out I didn't need to spend much of my day on the aforementioned tasks, as both were accomplished at the airport. I thought I'd need to go to the Immigration Bureau to extend my visa, and I'd booked a hotel room in the Intramuros district for the night so that I could spend all day paddling my way through the bureaucracy. But airport personnel pulled me aside during the immigration process and completed my visa process for me, for a $10 fee. In the airport lobby just beyond the little in-airport Immigration office, there was a booth selling Globe SIM cards along with a month's-worth of internet access at a discounted rate. I bought one, popped it in my phone, and wrote down my new phone number.

Missions accomplished, and way ahead of schedule.

It's a indication of some kind of progress that the easiest and cheapest way to get from an airport to a hotel in many big cities is Uber, the regional infrastructure almost everywhere quite clunky and corrupt by comparison. The ride-hailing service has been legal in the Philippines for a little while now, and though there were some hiccups along the way to fully legit status, all such issues were taken care of by the time I arrived. My driver was friendly, there was no haggling over whether or not he turned on the meter (an issue in many cities, where taxi drivers will often charge tourists hefty fees rather than the metered price they charge locals), and the twenty-minute drive to my hotel cost only four bucks. It definitely felt like progress.

I was planning to explore Intramuros that night, but was informed that in order to catch my bus the next day, I'd need to be awake and ready to go by four in the morning. This gave me just enough time to grab a bite near my hotel, stretch and work out a little to alleviate the worst of my flight-induced muscle kinks, and conk out around eight. I woke at three in the next morning, took a quick shower, and met my contact, who had hired a taxi to take us to the bus station.

The traffic in Manila is bad. When I lived in LA I couldn't imagine worse traffic from what I'd experienced there, but when you live in South America or Southeast Asia for a little while you begin to use a new scale for such things. It's a bit like switching over to a horrible, pollution-pumping, bumper-grinding metric system used for gauging the intensity of bad traffic.

Traffic in Bangkok was bad, traffic in Buenos Aires was bad, traffic in Kolkata was really bad, traffic in LA? Annoying. Not terrible. Manila, in my approximation, ranks somewhere between Bangkok and Kolkata. Not the worst I've ever experienced, but deplorable enough that it warrants leaving the city early if you want to get to the outskirts by early afternoon.

The bus would take me to Santiago City, where I would meet a contact from Mayoyao who would transport me the rest of the way. The bus was comfortable, air conditioned, and I got a window seat (yes!). The ride itself took about nine hours, and I mostly spaced out, read a book, and chatted in simple English with the little old lady in the seat next to mine.

It was early afternoon when I arrived in Santiago City, and I was instructed to wait at a nearby McDonald's. Like riding a bike, I segued into the 'crossing streets in Asia' mentality I learned while living in Thailand and India years before, which involves ignoring posted signs and working with the rhythm and flow of traffic, like a Frogger-dance that's most ideally performed without showing a hint of panic on your face or in your stride.

In many of the places I've lived, I've been the only Caucasian person for miles. I guessed this might not be the case in Manila, but there wasn't much tourism where I'd stayed, so the stares started the moment I disembarked the plane.

Something I learned while in Bangkok, and which was reinforced in Kolkata, is that staring isn't rude in much of the world. In the US, if you just sit and stare at someone and don't look away or nod or respond when they make eye contact with you, it's quite discourteous and a little disconcerting, maybe borderline threatening. In Asia it's mostly no big deal, and is a folkway you have to come to terms with if you want to be in public at all.

Walking into the McDonald's in Santiago City was comical: the whole place stopped, as if flash-frozen, as I walked up. Everyone turned to look at this white guy entering what amounts to a church of Western ideology. My only visits to McDonald's in the past five or ten years have been overseas, and this tends to be the response each time. Here we are in a food-slinging, cartoon version of America, and here's this guy, like a mascot of that culture, walking in like nothing abnormal is occurring. I ordered a coffee and sat in a corner, and three different groups, two mobs of teenagers and a family of diverse ages, surreptitiously took selfies, aiming their smartphone lenses so that I was in the background. I smiled a friendly photobomb each time before hunching back over my coffee.

The contact I was waiting for at the McDonald's was a woman named Florence, and as I understood it, she was in charge of the emerging tourism industry for Mayoyao. They don't get a lot of visitors in the region, due in part to lack of infrastructural amenities, and she was riding with a small caravan of people who were visiting Santiago City, which was the nearest town with an ATM and grocery store. I later learned that government employees who work in Mayoyao are paid with checks, and these checks must be brought someplace like Santiago City to be cashed because it's also the home of the closest bank. It's a three-hour trip each way.

Florence directed me to a local grocery store, where I picked up some ground coffee and shampoo. I didn't know exactly what amenities I would have at my soon-to-be home in Mayoyao, but I figured that these were two items I could probably procure without much risk of either going to waste. We then loaded into a pill-bug van, the kind that were popular in the US in the '70s, with nearly a dozen other people.

The van driver, I was told, hires his services to people who live in the small towns and settlements along the mountain roads. There are a few buses that cover the same route, but they take around six hours to get to Mayoyao from Santiago City, while the smaller van takes only three. Unless you have your own vehicle, this is the only way to get from these mountain-locked locations to a larger city. As we traveled, we passed many other vans, motorbikes with sidecars colloquially called 'trikes' (which in Bangkok would be called 'tuk-tuks' and in Kolkata would be called 'autos'), and what looked like big Jeeps, pulled by the snout and stretched to unlikely lengths (locals call these 'jeepneys'). Passengers were piled high and wide, occupying all vehicular surfaces and handholds, and most of the vehicles themselves were decorated elaborately. It was like driving through a dystopian steampunk future at times, as many of the vehicles looked to be cobbled together from whatever parts were at hand, and some were stylized like nightclubs or spaceships or giant acorns or other unidentifiable but chaotic and interesting shapes.

The roads were a disaster. Some were paved, but the farther into the mountains we went, the more they were made out of dirt and rocks and hope. The rocks varied in size, from that of a fist to that of a basketball, and they seemed to be all that held the dirt in place, and only just barely. There was intermittent rain that turned everything to mud, rivulets and waterfalls pouring down the mountainside, sometimes splashing over the van, sometimes just a beautiful, possibly dangerous view along the way. There were landslides and rockslides and mudslides; slides of all kinds tumbling whatever was above us, higher up the mountain, down onto our road, reducing the already tight one-and-a-half-lane width into something more like three-fourths.

Though driving habits in the Philippines are frantic by US standards, I actually felt much safer on those mountain roads than I often do in big cities within the States. In the US, people tend to obey traffic laws and posted signs, while here such things seem more like suggestions that are casually ignored. That said, many Filipinos seem to drive with a well-honed reflex that turns the chaos into a synchronized activity. Yes, we're flying straight toward a semi-truck, and yes, we're passing jeepnies and trikes with less than an inch between us. But the system of friendly and informative honks, combined with the driver's comfort and skill with sudden stops and quick accelerations means that everyone gets where they need to go with minimal hand-wringing. It's a system based on acting rationally in the moment and adhering to common sense, which contrasts with the Western ideal of creating a system of rules and regulations that are meant to keep drivers from having to make individual decisions. Both models have pros and cons, but this approach to driving makes sense for areas like this, where modern technology is built atop outdated infrastructure in an imperfect, unblended way. It's an elegant solution to a problem that would otherwise cause a lot more trouble than it does.

We were perhaps twenty minutes from Mayoyao when we careened around a curve to find the back of a massive truck looming over us. We were at a steep incline, as we had been for a while, and the driver jumped out to see what was the matter. There weren't many people who spoke English in the van, and they were way in the back, so most of what was happening I had to figure out based on body-language and gestures. But it was pretty clear that we were stopped and would remain stopped for a time. There were a handful trucks and buses ahead of our van, stretching across the space leading to the next turn in the road, and I later found out that there had been a massive mudslide a few bends ahead, blocking traffic along a strip of road that usually only had one lane to begin with.

We sat there for over an hour, and I watched the sun go down as perky country music from the '90s played optimistically from the van's radio. Fellow passengers left the vehicle periodically, and I was later told that they'd all helped clear the road, carving a traversable path through the mudslide. A group of people from the bus, from the trucks ahead of us, and folks from a nearby town all did what needed to be done because you can't just call someone else to come out and fix your problems when you live far from any city worth the label.

Eventually, the trucks and buses and vans started moving again, and our little van wobbled over the mountains of mud, a gaggle of sludge-caked people guiding us lurch-by-lurch, trying to ensure we didn't bottom out or pierce a tire on the sharp sticks jabbing out from the mud at irregular intervals.

Twenty minutes later, we were in Mayoyao. The worst of the rain waited for us to arrive, and began pouring down as soon as we exited the vehicle. I've never been happier to have packed an umbrella.

I was led to my home, which was a sprawling affair. It was meant to house a lot of people, but for the month I was visiting it would contain only me.

I woke up to the sound of roosters crowing and dogs barking and birds fluttering everywhere. I saw a cat prowling around while I sat on my balcony. I sipped coffee and took it all in.

The house was beautiful, the view spectacular. The balcony overlooked the town, hundreds of nearby native homes, and a valley lined with the famous, remarkable rice terraces that link the region together. That first day I had a half-dozen visitors, each introducing themselves and helping me get set up in some way: adjusting the solar panels, hauling containers of clean water, showing me the house's various amenities.

I could already tell that Mayoyao was a very different sort of place, and I couldn't wait to discover exactly what kind of different it might be.

MAYOYAO

BUGS

I am covered in aphids.

They're not actually aphids, though. Not triangular and bright green. The insects encrusting my every exposed surface are more like tiny grasshoppers, each about the size of a grain of rice, ranging in pallor from a light greenish-brown to a dark, dull gray.

Over the last few days, I've emerged from my room each morning to find not-aphid corpses coating the dining room table, but this morning their collective mass formed a crunchy, mostly dead shell along my arms, torso, and one of my legs which hadn't been properly covered by my bedsheets. There were some on my face but not so many as elsewhere, which leads to me to believe that either my breathing discouraged them from landing up there in the first place, or I spent the night inhaling entire generations of tiny bugs.

The caretakers of the house I'm renting here in Mayoyao are horrified by the presence of these bugs. They comment on them each time they bring a meal or stop by to clean the kitchen or the bathroom or to wash the linens.

After many years of travel I can quickly become accustomed to anything, and my reflex to fret over things in my environment has been sanded away. In some places there are bugs. In others there are lots of bugs. In very few places are there no bugs. Complaining about the relative bugginess of a place won't change anything. There's no reason to get upset about something that's as certain as the sun rising or the water boiling at a specific temperature.

Some things are changeable, though. The caretakers line the gaps in the window screens with Scotch tape and tear off long strips to cover the space along the bottom of the back door. They install a screen door upstairs, inside the massive, wooden double-doors that reveal a sprawling balcony that overlooks the magical, rice terrace-filled valley below. Scattered throughout the rows of rice are stair-step staggered native homes, built in the clever all-wood, socketed style their ancestors developed and perfected; a style replicated today in the newer models which utilize corrugated metal roofs instead of the dried-and-woven grass-tops that were more common up until a few decades ago. Old and new, their pyramidal tops point to the sky, poking up from the agrarian landscape like chess pieces in tall grass.

This area has been continuously settled, the rice terraces continuously worked, for over two thousand years. The expansive terraces, sprawling astride the landscape in this valley and all nearby valleys, are a UNESCO Heritage Site, treasured for their history and what they tell us about a radically different age.

In the year zero of the Gregorian calendar, the ancestors of these residents, the ones who smilingly tape my windows and door gaps against not-aphids, worked these terraces and fed their families, same as the people who live here today. They eat the rice produced, they slaughter local hogs and chickens, they feed the neighborhood dogs scraps and shoo away the odd cat who lingers too close to the pantry.

In a place like this, the bugs are like motes of dust: tiny grains that add realism to a chemically exposed photograph displayed on ancient film. They are the Instagram filter that makes life appear realer than real, showing imperfections where you might otherwise only see smoothed out, even-toned skin, perfect hair with no fly-aways, and a smile that's whiter than unprinted photo paper. The imperfections are what one travels to see, to experience, to understand. Even when those imperfections are terrifying.

I have a friend who's scared of moths. I remember thinking, when I learned this about him, that it was a completely irrational fear. Moths are harmless, the manatee of the air. They're bumbling stunt pilots that may bump into you, but the chances of them harming you in any way are so slim as to be almost incalculable.

I finally understood this fear, though, after I met my first cockroach. It's remarkable that it's taken me so long to share a room with one of these giant filth beetles; I don't think I even had one scamper over my foot in a subway terminal until I was in college. Cockroaches are persistent, resilient, unwelcome roommates throughout much of the world, but I spent my childhood in the Midwest, where, although cockroaches exist, they tend to be shoved aside, outcompeted for space and attention by the myriad other horrors that lurk in every corner and crevice. You're less likely to notice an errant cockroach when you're shaking your sheets each night to scare away black widows and brown recluses, shuffling your feet to ward off copperheads, and staying mostly inside to avoid the hornets, yellow jackets, mosquitos of varying size, deer ticks, fire ants, black bears, skunks, rats, disease-carrying bats, badgers, bobcats, western pygmy rattlesnakes, tarantulas, wasps, assassin bugs, coyotes, millipedes, centipedes, wolf spiders, and the shockingly asshole-ish raccoon. Yes, cockroaches were one ingredient in that horrible nature-stew, but I was far more aware of the pokey, poisonous, toothy, kill-me-for-fun beasties that were far more pertinent when I was a kid.

The first cockroach I encountered here in Mayoyao was hanging out in the bathroom, clinging to the toilet.

When you notice any bug that's larger than a domino, it takes a moment for your brain to register what you're seeing. There's a deep-seated oh-hell-no reflex that typically involves staggering backward and assessing the situation from a safe distance, because this thing you're looking at occupies a higher-than-reasonable place on the size-spectrum for a bug. Because of its breadth, it dimensionally scuttle-walks into the realm of lizards, mammals, and fish. These animals have brains, maybe spines, and probably some kind of advanced circulatory system. They're worthy of, if not the same politeness and consideration offered to a fellow human being, or even a camelid, dog, horse, or other human-scale creature, at least more than what's offered to an ant or flea.

If the beastie is big enough to move your stuff around when you're not home, however, it's more 'real' than a bug that sees your socks as mountains and your stairs as insurmountable rice terraces.

This cockroach triggered my 'this is an animal' response because it was chunky and had a presence. It responded to me like a dog might respond: it watched me, it moved when I moved. It seemed to wonder if I could see it. If it should hold stock still until I passed. It seemed capable of making decisions based on how it thought I thought. A meta-bug.

When my brain was finally clear about what I was looking at, an involuntary shiver rippled through my body and I staggered back into the living room to grab a shoe with which to crush the monster. That was a few days ago. First blood in the cockroaches-versus-Colin rivalry went to me.

There are many other bugs invading my space that I'm not at all concerned about. But the cockroaches…when I see one, I usually shout something violent and strangely indignant, like, "Oh nuh uh, you bastard," before flailing around, trying to crush it with any flat-bottomed bludgeoning weapon within arm's reach.

I don't know where this reflex came from, compulsively acting as if these beetles are somehow personally insulting me by being here, as if their presence is an affront that cannot be tolerated. It's not fear, because I know rationally that they literally cannot hurt me. But my intense level of startlement surprises me every single time.

I woke up in the middle of the night yesterday and noticed a thumb-sized shadow in the window. I pulled on my glasses and could see that there was a cockroach clinging to the thin curtains covering my bedside window. It was silhouetted by the light shining in from outside, and its proximity to me, a slumbering me, without my clothes on, the curtain upon which it perched brushing against my sheets, had me catapulting out of bed, grabbing a shoe, and slamming it repeatedly against the shadow. This knocked the roach off the curtain and onto my bed, where it was squashed, posthaste.

My heart was racing, and I felt the now-familiar pissed-off, how-dare-you-come-into-my-home chemical cocktail stuttering its way through my bloodstream as I retreated to the bathroom for some toilet paper to clean the wee demon's guts from my sheets, shaking my head even then, wondering why this particular species triggers such a strong defense mechanism in me.

I can only imagine my friend's moth aversion is something similar. These creatures flutter their way into his life, disrupt his space, send his body's combat system into the same paroxysms he might get during a home invasion or while facing off against a saber-toothed tiger. And all he can do is wonder why, knowing full well that even if he comes up with an answer it won't do a thing to save the life of the next moth unfortunate enough to flit within swatting range.

Though it was nothing compared to what I've experienced elsewhere, there was an impressive representation by the local ant community waiting to greet me when I first arrived at the house here in Mayoyao. They would boldly strut into the kitchen, into the living room, into the bathroom, and grab something far too large for them to carry. They'd then tip their little hats my way and goose-step back out the door.

They were incredibly polite, for ants. Compared to the other bugs in residence, they were unobtrusive and kept to themselves. There was an ever-present stream of them heading somewhere, stealing something, yes, but I could see this well-organized crowd of tiny thieves and avoid them, as if they were, as a mass, something like a shy cat or awkwardly placed rock I could easily avoid stepping on. Their bulk was sometimes in the way, but it wasn't difficult to walk around or over them, so they never became a conscious concern. They were like a quiet, hungry roommate made up of tiny insects instead of skin cells and sinew.

The caretakers weren't having it, though. They brought in little trays of concrete and wall putty and filled in all the cracks in the walls, all the exposed seams under the kitchen counters, all the little holes that had gone unnoticed until the ants started using them as their primary mode of ingress. This has gone on for weeks. The flood of formic bodies will be staunched for a few days, but then flows afresh as their larger, outdoor hive-self readjusts to the changed architectural reality and discovers a new injection point.

For the last week, the ants have disappeared almost completely. The most I see of them are tiny scouts, separated from their standard stampede.

The other day I noticed a pair of ant workers tugging a moth wing behind them, the wing itself about twenty times bigger than their bodies. But the weight didn't phase them, and it didn't seem to scare them even a little.

I wondered if they handled cockroaches, as well.

TIME IS RELATIVE

Time is a finicky creature, less predictable than one of only four proven dimensions should be. It's also far less appreciated and respected than its more concrete siblings, length, width, and depth.

Consider that there is such a thing as absolute time. You might measure the radiation half-life of a particle, for instance. The amount of time it takes for an unstable atom to decay to half its original size will be the same no matter who's watching it. This is a fixed unit of data.

When we talk about time, we typically use a less definitive temporal yardstick. Time zones carve up the planet into unevenly cut pieces, defined in some cases by lines of longitude, in others by national border, government mandate, or geographic convenience. Some countries, or segments of a country, like certain US states, ignore Daylight Savings Time, which is a commonly accepted deviation in this system. Whether they're crazy, or those who accept regular government-mandated shifts in time are the nutty ones, it's difficult to say.

My perception of time can change how I measure it, and that perception can be influenced by pretty much anything.

When I fly from one country to another, and my destination is twelve or thirteen time zones away, it's possible that I'll arrive at the exact same time that I left, and on the exact same day. It's equally possible that I'll lose a day completely: though only ten hours of absolute time have passed, I may arrive twenty hours later in terms of how time is measured by society.

The logistics and conception of time can be disorienting because very often nothing has changed other than your position in the world, and that is something most ideally measured by those other three dimensions.

Despite the erratic relationship we have with it, time impacts the way we interact with the world.

When I'm living in the US, I'm aware of who's awake, where. If I'm in the Midwest, for instance, I know that people in New York are probably waking up perhaps an hour before me, and going to sleep an hour earlier. My friends in Seattle are two hours behind. If I'm scheduling something to be published online, I take these time differences into consideration. I may try to schedule it so that I reach New Yorkers around lunch and Seattleites just after they've arrived at work. Hitting everyone at once, however, is impossible. There are just too many simultaneous states of being to consider, and these states are determined by our relative experience of time.

While living in another country, in a far removed time zone, other concerns come into play. When I wake up in the morning in the Philippines, the people I'm most accustomed to interacting with online are having dinner and thinking about going to sleep. When I'm getting ready for bed, US residents are waking up, having breakfast, and going to work. Again, time hasn't changed, but my experience of it, particularly in relation to how other people experience it, has changed. Our perceptions of time are misaligned.

If you operate globally, such a shift forces you to reassess your entire schedule. Is relative-time alignment with those in another part of the world vital enough for you to stay up late or get up super-early? Or are bookend touchpoints sufficient to maintain important relationships and accomplish whatever it is you hope to achieve by staying in touch?

In such circumstances you also find yourself quite suddenly synced with a new group of people. A whole chunk of the human population with whom you've been unable to conveniently communicate in the past is now waking when you wake, eating approximately when you eat. What can you accomplish, now, freshly time-aligned with this regional sub-set of your species? How might you interact with them, reach out and introduce yourself? And how else might you spend your time, lacking those other, now-defunct daily interactions in which you no longer partake? Disconnected from both routine and a localized perception of time, how best to spend the free hours you've gained? How might you recalibrate your day to accept this new reality, and benefit from it?

Here in Mayoyao, my day is divided up into three time segments, the borders between these fragments defined by my meals.

My mornings are for mugs of black coffee, brewed in a pot that came with the house I'm renting, consumed primarily on the balcony overlooking a rice terrace-laced valley and its accompanying mountains. During these soft-glow hours I catch up with the world beyond my backyard, periodically staring off into the distance, thinking those deep thoughts that are only possible when you're left well-enough alone in your reverie. These moments lead into my connecting to millions of other people around the world via social media, by tweeting and Facebooking and newslettering. I've been playing with an app called Periscope which allows me to shoot a live video feed from my phone. I'll sometimes share my morning gazing-into-the-distance moments with people from around the world through this platform, which is another interesting deviation from the norm.

At around one in the afternoon, after many hours of caffeine and writing and interacting with the still-awake population beyond the mountains of Mayoyao's Ifugao region, I'm presented with a meal prepared by a neighbor who is a masterful cook. Most of these meals include a large pile of sticky rice alongside a few dishes, ranging from soups to heaps of veggies to well-seasoned meats. Some of the dishes I've been served include the traditional chicken or pork adobo, fish dumplings, a type of stew called *kare-kare*, pinoy pork steak, *misua* rice noodle soup, boiled beef with *pechay* leaves, a dish consisting of sautéed sweet potato tops called *ginisang talbos ng kamote*, squash cream soup, a sweet dish called pork *tocino*, *ginisang malunggay* leaves, chicken curry, fish flakes with pineapple sauce, a fish cake-laden soup called *odeng*, a small meatloaf wrapped around a hard-boiled egg called *embutido*, *bola-bola* meatballs, a ginger and onion-based soup called *tinola*, varied preparations of *bangus*, also known as milkfish, a beef soup with bok choy called *nilagang baka*, a sour meat soup called pork *sinigang* with rattan fruit, *giniling guisado*, which combines pork and bell peppers in a tomato sauce, breaded french beans, crab and corn soup, steamed monggo sprouts with orche peas in sesame oil, a dish that combines okra, *talong* (eggplant), *pechay* (a Chinese cabbage), and a chili pepper called *sili haba* in a cumin sauce, squash balls, and my personal favorite, a common breakfast dish called *longsilog*, which derives its name from its three ingredients: *longganisa* (Filipino sausage), *sinangag* (garlic fried rice), and *itlog* (egg).

Next comes my second day-segment, the hours after lunch and leading up to dinner, which arrives each day at seven in the evening.

During this period I write, I read, I wander around town and meander through the rice terraces. This chunk of time is at least partially defined by the social silence I enjoy, as the US is asleep and I am awake. Knowing this, I feel both panicked and liberated. I wonder what I'm missing, what shared experiences I'm not a part of, what cultural events are passing me by in my chronological absence. But I'm also free. I feel more comfortable spending my time alone, here, in this moment, completely untethered from those beneficial but insidious tendrils of the worldwide human network. The sights, sounds, tastes, and interactions within range of my own biological instruments are the only inputs available. Though I often disentangle myself from the internet throughout the day, regardless, it's a far easier habit to keep when the people you most frequently interact with are asleep, and when most of the websites and feeds published in your language are stagnant.

Dinner is the same as lunch: delicious. I'm presented with more rice, with bowls of *ginataang sigarilyas* (winged beans in coconut milk), *gisadong orche* peas with pork strips, *malunggay* in oyster sauce, *inihaw na liempo* (grilled pork belly), and *sitaw* and *kalabasa* (green beans and squash) in coconut milk.

The food sets the tone for my night. During my evenings in Mayoyao I spend more time consuming than producing, reading while I digest or laying around, anaconda-like, listening to podcasts. Before I left for Southeast Asia I realized that I was largely uneducated about film, so I've also been working my way through a list of what are considered by some to be the best movies ever made. As a result, most of my evenings are spent indulging in amazing Filipino food while watching classics like The Godfather, Modern Times, Rear Window, or Apocalypse Now.

It's remarkable how much novelty influences our perception of time.

Our brains orient us toward activities and thought processes which consume the least amount of energy. Which makes a lot of sense, evolutionarily, because you never know when you'll need some spare glucose in the tank for an emergency spear-making or tiger-escaping scenario. This predilection carries over to today, the consequence being that many of our daily habits are put on autopilot, which conserves valuable thought-fueling energy that needn't be wasted on familiar movements, experiences, and interactions.

As a result of this routine-building predisposition, we barely notice the drive to work, and sometimes find ourselves looking up from the steering wheel, already at the office parking lot and unable to recall the specifics of how we got there. The drive that we make every day becomes so reflexive that our brain doesn't even bother to notify us that it happened.

This automation goes far beyond commuting. We listen to the same, familiar music, have the same conversations with well-known, comfortable friends, loop through the same meal-time, bed-time, and after-work habits that we've been repeating for months, years, perhaps decades. It's no surprise that time compresses under these circumstances. So much of our day is rote, processed and accomplished without requiring our brain's active attention. At some point it's not the parking lot that we notice when we look up from the steering wheel, but life. We're here, experiencing this point in time, but unsure of how we got here. Where did all those years go? Why doesn't anything from the time between 'now' and 'back then' stand out?

Time doesn't fly, it's just automated into obscurity.

In contrast, by waking the brain up, forcing it to pay attention, we are aware for a greater portion of our lives. Rather than spending only half of each day conscious of what we're doing, we can experience the entirety of our waking hours: alert and forming memories and making intentional decisions.

Achieving this requires a dramatic shift in lifestyle and priority, however. One must be willing to grab one's mind by the shoulders and slap it across the face any time it starts to get blurry or lose interest. This requires that we expose ourselves to novelty with greater frequency. It's not enough to want to be awake and alive, we have to show the brain that it needs to regularly expend energy on paying attention. We have to retrain our brains toward vigilance. Learning promotes this type of activity. So do novel experiences, fixating on details, new relationships, and identifying relationships between disparate things and ideas.

Travel is perhaps the simplest way to achieve this mindset regularly, because while in-transit, you're barraged with unfamiliar stimuli — language, smells, colors, foods, ideas, perspectives — and jolted out of comfort zones whether you want to be or not. Frequent travel is an excellent way to automate lifestyle non-automation.

You needn't become nomadic to maintain intellectual consciousness, of course. Regularly taste-testing new music or genres of books, reaching out to non-adjacent social circles and making new friends with different backgrounds, beliefs, and lifestyles, and even recognizing that you know little about something, like movies, and then going out of your way to learn about that field, that craft, that industry, and that study can factor positively into how oriented toward alertness your brain becomes.

Keeping your mind active, not allowing it to go into sleep mode, is what gives you access to more of your time each and every day, and makes each minute, each hour, each month, each year, seem densely packed with life. It allows you to look back on what you've done and say, "Stuff happened."

It also allows you to look toward your future with excitement, safe in the assumption that there will be plenty going on, confident that you can truthfully add, "And more stuff will happen."

IRRESPONSIBLE

I'm paying close attention. Almost always, I'm noticing.

This hasn't always been the case. This hyper-aware sense for perhaps-meaningless, uninformative things in my environment is the result of long-term travel.

When you're in another place, immersed in another culture, experiencing a lifestyle different from the one that you're most comfortable and familiar with, you're bombarded with answers, but also questions.

Why does their economy work this way? Why do people tilt their head in that way when greeting a friend? Why is the most prominent shade of blue in the paints they use a slightly greener shade that what I'm accustomed to?

There are any number of reasons for these things, and more often than not our first answer, the obvious answer, is incorrect or incomplete. Pushing past the easy answers, the obvious ones, is part of the challenge. Taking in more information, expanding your context, that's the ultimate goal.

In recent years a trend for well-cultivated mustaches worn by young men has reemerged in many different cultures. This was a hip style years ago, and decades ago, and generations ago; it's cyclical. A style that pops up to enjoy an occasional few years in the sun before retreating in favor the clean-shaven look once more. Facial hair of the upper-lip is in, then once more becomes the wheelhouse of older gentlemen and the odd-duck youngster.

At the moment, the trend prevails as a result of a global nostalgia amongst the middle- and upper-economic classes. In the US, you see a lot of the whimsical waxed-and-curled-up variety, a look that references and lampoons traditional masculinity and is aligned with simultaneous movements in fashion, food, and body art.

In the Philippines, though, the more dominant trend is for downward-slanting mustaches. Here, the hip youth prefer facial hair that wraps down the cheeks like a horseshoe, rather than the kind that's pulled upward, waxed against gravity. A hair frown rather than a hair smile.

Encountering this in a vacuum, one would be hard-press to find a reason for the sudden resurgence of this specific facial decoration. Taken in context, however, there are a variety of reasons, all of them equally valid in assessing the movement and its sudden reappearance.

The play on traditionally masculinity is certainly a factor. It's very 'in' to display the trappings of gender normativity that our grandparents' generation would recognize, but with a modern twist.

The historical context is that the downward-curved mustache — though less traditional in the East Coast of the US, a place where many of these new nostalgia trends have been born and then pushed out into the world — was quite common in other cultures, including Asia. It's a more US Western cowboy look, and that aspect of historical masculine culture has flourished in all corners of the planet.

The physical context is that most people in the Philippines have thick, shiny, black hair. This hair type behaves differently that the Caucasian hair that is more common elsewhere in the mustache-relevant world, and as such Filipino facial hair is more easily cultivated into a horseshoe mustache than the upward-curved variety.

There's also the economic context. The wax required to create some of the more gravity defying mustache creations may not be as readily available in the Philippines. In the places like the US, where just about anything can be ordered and delivered the next day, it's easy to forget that this is not the case in most of the rest of the world. That a trend might not manifest because the proper consumer components for that trend are unavailable is quite likely.

When I travel, I try to pay attention to what's going on around me, even the minor details, because when I guess about why something might be a certain way, I'm often wrong. Or almost certainly wrong. I can't know for sure until later, until I know far more and have more context, and even then there's a chance that I missed something or wasn't exposed to the right stimuli or variables to get all the answers.

There's a humility to this process that makes you question everything you think you know. You come to realize that no matter how tight your arguments and explanations seem, the likelihood of being wrong due to ignorance is such an ever-present possibility that you temper your words with 'probably's and 'maybe's and 'I think's all the time.

A key part of the traveling experience is leaving yourself

open to possibilities you can't imagine yet and recognizing that there are many unknowns you'll likely never know. But you still scramble to find as many of them as possible, despite that knowledge. You try to see the world of ignorance as a wealth of possibilities rather than a threat. This is a state of mind that beneficially carries over into life as a whole, by the way, not only your knowledge-seeking wanderings.

We all have a different level of tolerance for unpredictability and incomprehension. Some of us have a tolerance that is almost a need: we require novelty and a regular dollop of confusion and disorientation to feel complete. We need to have our world set spinning so that we can ever so slowly bring it back to a more regular rotation on a sturdy axis.

Another way to look at this is that the more you travel, the more you find predictability in even the most foreign, unfamiliar, confounding-as-hell situations and environments.

The varied social structures and habits, the architecture and stylistic preferences, the politeness and politics, the means of value exchange and methods of survival, they're different in ways great and small everywhere you go, but you begin to notice commonalities. Even if the connection between two places, two people, two cultures is a tenuous one, barely noticeable with the naked eye, you see the similarities despite the overwhelming differences.

Over time, this tendency becomes a core part of a person. To see what we share, how similar we all are. Even though you haven't met someone before, you can recognize in them attributes shared by your friends, your family, yourself. Even though you haven't been to a certain city before, you can imagine why people stay here, why they visit and long for this place once they've moved on, because you do the same with other places that have some of the same attributes.

This habit creates a red thread that weaves through every person and every place you encounter, so that rather than merely collecting an expansive diversity of ideas and colors and tastes and cultural norms, you're also building a mental model that shows you how even the most disparate groups are connected, and how even the most long-standing conflicts stem from a shared set of histories, values, and ideologies.

Imagine, then, how this makes a person who travels feel about novelty. About new places, new homes, new people in their lives. How that feeling feeds their enthusiasm about new technologies, new artistic movements, new foods prepared at a restaurant they haven't tried before. These unfamiliar things cease to be scary, cease to be threatening in the way that unknowns can be, because we're able to recognize in them something familiar. A touchpoint that grounds the idea, novel as it might seem, in the concrete. It makes imagining next steps and possibilities a practical act, rather than an idealistic, nebulous daydream.

Travel, particularly long-term travel, can seem like an irresponsible thing. It can appear from the outside to be the act of an overwhelmed person fleeing from life, from responsibility, from the difficulties of the real world. It can be considered desperate, as if one who travels cannot cope with what life has to offer and therefore must go out and pursue a fantasy land, something different from the familiar. New for the sake of new.

This is typically a wildly inaccurate perception. Travel requires discipline in how a person spends their time and their money. Managing work, relationships, habits, and needs are all more difficult from the road, not simpler. One loose thread can mean the end of your entire lifestyle, so diligence and self-accountability are absolutely essential at all times.

The main difference is that while traveling we're responsible for ourselves. Rather than having someone else crack the whip over our heads, we have to make it to the airport on time all by lonesome, with no consequences other than missing the plane if we fail to arrive before the gate closes. We are responsible for our own happiness and our own entertainment.

People who approach this type of lifestyle expecting it to solve all their problems tend to wash out pretty quickly, heading back to a more predictable system, with regulations and routines established by someone else. Travel is not an activity for those who refuse to be accountable for themselves.

You have to look around, see challenges, and smile. You have to cram yourself into small spaces, be hauled across vast distances, and re-inflate to your full size on the other side, excited to start exploring. You have to be open to the possibility, even the probability, that you will be the most ignorant person in the room nearly all the time and use that fact to your advantage.

Travel provides the chance to think, to work, to learn, to experience, to process, to spread one's wings, to relax, to be pushed up against one's limitations, to work every muscle in one's body and mind, to feel uncomfortable and grow accustomed to the feeling. It's the chance to see horizons you didn't know existed, and to crest those horizons.

And then, when all you see is three new horizons where you were hoping to find answers, you start moving in some direction, knowing what will happen when you get to another crest, knowing each victory only unlocks new challenges, but looking forward to the journey anyway.

DARK AND LOUD

The darkness is absolute, but the sound is cacophonic.

Cricket-sounding bugs chirp news of their prowess at anyone who'll listen, while something else — another, bulkier bug? a tiny, baritone frog? — drones tirelessly, adding its voice to the complex nighttime ensemble that sings each night like a chorus of micro-scale Buddhist monks.

Using my phone as a flashlight, I climb the stairs and step out onto the balcony. Here, there are gradients to the blackness. Blues and grays, slates and wisps of powdery white. The clouds have rolled in and over the town, blocking out the reflected light of the moon and glimmery sparkle of the stars. A luminary challenge is typically offered by the windows filtering lamp glow from the many small houses speckling the landscape, clinging to the mountainside, and perched upon the earth-scale stairway of rice terraces, but when a brownout descends at night, no lights pierce the darkness. Except for the rare, unquenched cookfire somewhere within shouting range, even from way up here the only light comes from my phone.

When I turn the phone off, though, I notice another dim glow off in the distance. I can only see it because I know where to look, its luster faint because of its location five or six miles away. One of the summit-roosting antennas that provide mobile phone signals for the area has a generator so that even during these frequent power failures the town remains connected to the internet. The light is a visual representation of that connection: we're still here, it says. Even now we're part of a larger human ecosystem.

It's an unusual feeling, experiencing absolute optical isolation while still remaining in complete, perhaps too-frequent contact with the outside world. The visual spectrum, typically my main source of environmental information, is rendered useless for anything except what I can glean from the surface of a phone, a laptop, or backlit ebook reader. These devices become a lifeline, a tenuous tunnel to information from a well-wired world beyond my view, beyond the scope of these mountains, but one more achievable, more relatable and understandable than even the balcony rail two feet in front of me, the house behind and below me, and the town just outside my front door.

The sound of the perhaps-crickets and maybe-frogs overwhelm the audible spectrum, rendering my ears near-useless, while the lack of light achieves for my eyes the same purpose in reverse.

There are lightning flashes on the horizon, periodically illuminating the mountains that I know are there, pulling them out in stark contrast to the dark night sky, shrouded as it is, concealing as it is, foreboding as it is. In a situation such as this, lighting becomes an object of hope rather than a fearful thing; becomes an optical connection to something real.

It's important to have hobbies which don't require electricity to enjoy. It's only when the lights are gone that this becomes clear, that it becomes obvious just how easily the things you enjoy, the activities in which you engage to keep yourself entertained and growing, can be pulled out of reach.

At night, at least, books are out of the question. An ebook reader with a light will keep you going for a time, but only for a time, and only if you remembered to charge it. Music, too, is dependent on some device's battery, on portable electricity. Such gadgets remain functional when everything else has blipped beyond operability, but for how long? If you don't know when you'll be able to re-juice your tech, are any chip-based, post-Industrial Revolution technologies long-term, safe options?

The laptop, typically a workhorse and the place where I do most of my writing, internet surfing, and less productive activities, is a clear point of weakness. Not chargeable via USB, and as such not as easily re-energized as a phone or other small device. I typically close my computer and pack it away as soon as the lights go out, saving it for a more vital moment.

The phone becomes, primarily, a flashlight during these moments. It's my contact with the outside world, my guide around the forest of previously easy-to-avoid pitfalls scattered around my house. It's the easiest of my devices to recharge, and can be fed to capacity through a portable battery pack. This makes it incredibly useful and reliable in the post-electricity world in which I find myself several times a week.

Rather than stress over the death of my gizmos and habits, when the electricity flickers out I usually sit quietly in the dark, listening to the chirps and chants and barks, the occasional confused rooster who's not sure what's going on but wants to add his voice to the mix, to my own breathing, to the thoughts I usually shove aside in favor of more pertinent things. I sit in the dark and sift through details about something that happened ten years ago or something that may happen ten years hence.

I focus on the here, the now, my leg falling asleep, the subtle shades and shadows that emerge around the room as my eyes begin to adjust to the darkness, to a world without light.

The room, my life, is dark and loud, and though lacking the same potential it had before the world around me disappeared, the lights sputtering and stuttering and then deciding to give up the ghost, it still contains a sort of magic. As if this moment into which I accidentally stumbled, a moment in which my eyes have been made worthless, my hearing superhuman, itself contains something underutilized or untapped. Some promise of recognition or realization, some internal power untapped and unappreciated..

I met a designer from Poland while I was living in Iceland, and he complained to me that Americans have a natural advantage in the design world. In much of Europe there are excessive taxes, import fees, and other costs adhered to most electronics, and as such something like a computer monitor can cost nearly twice as much as it does Stateside. The context of his complaint made me think, at the time, that he was tasting sour grapes. His business wasn't flourishing the way he had hoped, so he conveniently blamed his lack of paying clientele on his inability to procure an affordable computer monitor.

Looking back at that conversation, though, I think he was probably on to something. Perhaps this isn't always true — it's debatable whether or not having a specific monitor will allow you to attain more clients — but the build-up over time of one's comfort level with technology is sure to influence one's work and how one reaches out to new, potential customers. Having always had access to relatively inexpensive professional-grade laptops, for instance, meant that back when I sustained myself by doing branding work for clients, I could be more selective about who I did business with, and could get started on higher-end work earlier in my career. I didn't have to spend too much time saving to procure the right tools for the job.

On a broader scale, imagine what an advantage it is to grow up with the internet, to have always had access to the web, to app stores, to mobile connectivity. To have a decent familiarity with extra-continental communication even before you can tie your shoes.

In Mayoyao, I've had three different people comment on how nice my phone is. How thin, how fast, how beautiful. In the US where I purchased it, my phone is middling at best; a cheaper model that allows me to do my work and stay in touch with my friends and family, but not so expensive that I would cry if it fell into a rice terrace or were run over by a jeepney. In some ways, though, my lower-end phone is one of the most capable computers in the whole town. It definitely outpaces the laptops and desktops I've seen in offices and homes, and much of the population uses the type of ten-year-old feature phone you can't even find in the US anymore, outside of antique malls and eBay.

It's true, of course, that talent is talent. There are some remarkably intelligent and capable people in Mayoyao, and there are many skills that exist here, and which are artfully practiced, which elsewhere have been rendered inessential by technology.

But in the modern world, an age in which we're all tied together in some way, in which forest fires in Indonesia cause an uptick in cancers in Singapore, and the price of tea in China can startle the stock exchange in the US, a familiarity with technology is more than just a nice thing to have. It's become a must-have trait for employees in almost every industry you can imagine, and those who lack such skills — the elderly, the impoverished, those with religious convictions that compel them to avoid anything that uses electricity — are at a substantial disadvantage when it comes to earning, and thereby participating in the global economy. These are people, then, who are not just handicapped in terms of operating locally, they're also voiceless in the groundbreaking conversations that are happening around the world, between people of every other possible group.

The technologically voiceless are in some ways the most invisible among us. Hoping to be heard, to participate, but speaking a language too antiquated to be noticed by those of us who speak in tweets, through hashtags, with spurts of emoji, utilizing crypto-locked SMSes, using ironic GIFs, with viral videos, and on devices so fast and inexpensive that we wouldn't even know how to operate something a decade older and ten million times less powerful, such as the ones so many people around the world still use daily.

I sometimes challenge myself to imagine a world in which modern technology, all the things I take for granted, are gone. They've disappeared overnight.

Setting aside the obvious worldwide economic, governmental, and military considerations, what would I do as an individual? How would my life change? How would I make a living and entertain myself? How would I regain contact with all the people with whom I'm able to stay in touch so casually online? Would I be able to reconnect with the audience I've accrued over the years? Would someone with skills like mine even be capable of doing valuable work in a disconnected, tech-less economy, or would I be relegated to the 'noncomplex manual labor' division, useful only for digging ditches and other menial tasks?

The skills we don't use atrophy, and as the world becomes more automated, more friction-free, a lot of the mental and physical muscles our parents and their parents used regularly have become less useful despite being mighty. Were the tech-centric system to collapse, however, those who have maintained their outdated muscles would be valuable beyond belief. In a world in which the global technological infrastructure has disappeared, a town full of people who are well-versed in building nail- and metal-free houses with local materials, and who can harvest all the food they need locally, are gods among men. They are self-sustaining seeds of productivity that could allow the species to propagate, even if civilization as we know it ceases to exist.

Those who live in places where the electricity is faulty, the roads are not reliable, and the internet is still a new thing to get excited about are working with muscles that aren't fully developed. They're competing in a sport with rules they don't fully understand that uses equipment they can't acquire, and playing against a team for whom the game is everything and is played from birth.

Being forced into an world opposite from that which one grew up in can be disorienting, even traumatizing. It can be stressful and strenuous and requires the same training and slow build-up as working muscles that have never been used.

For me, trying to survive in a post-apocalyptic, agrarian society, would be more than daunting. For a farmer who grew up in a remote area in the mountains, excluded from many of the developments of the past hundred years, not to mention the last twenty, having the larger, interconnected, largely electrical and silicon-based world foisted upon you must be frustrating, uncomfortable, and at times infuriating.

That the people of Mayoyao take to technology with not just patience, but enthusiasm, is a marvel to me. That they admire other people's smartphones and go out of their way to learn how to use unfamiliar social networks, that they embrace the world beyond their borders while also appreciating and maintaining that which they've long held dear within their own society, is remarkable.

It's hard to say what will happen in the coming years in places where high-end consumer technology meets traditional ways of life and vice versa, and where electrified, neon cities find that embracing some anthropological traditions may be not just beneficial, but necessary if they're to be prepared for the worst and primed for the best.

Either way, there's a lot we can learn from each other, and when our resources are pooled we're far more rugged and sustainable as a global culture, and as a species.

BIOMES

My allergies may be killing me.

I'm sapped of energy, drained of motivation. My eardrums are muffled with cotton and my cranium is over-pressurized. My eyes itch beyond what seems reasonable, almost to the point of being painful, or pleasurable, or post-scratch but not quite; on the precipice of something else, teetering between 'so extreme it's relatively easy to ignore' and 'so extreme I can't think of anything else.'

I don't rub my eyes, because down that road there is nothing but madness. Irritating an allergy-infused orifice is one of the worst decisions a person can make, on a cost-benefit level. Better to allow the feeling to ebb and flow, to settle and periodically puff up in a cloud of histamine. Allow your nose to run, sprint, break the sound barrier, and your throat to somehow be both dry and drowning in cough-inducing fluid, an esophagial superposition that flips first one way, then the other, reversing its function as soon as you're lucky enough to become numb to its state.

My first week in Mayoyao was punctuated by Noah-grade rainstorms, complete with flashbulb lightning and thunder that vibrated through my body like a cheap massage chair. After that week, the rain has become sparse. The thirsty flora, having chugged all that water, is detonating pollen bombs like it's the last day of a war.

This whole town is intertwined with jungle, bricolaged with agriculture, and tucked into the few, cozy, convenient spaces between mountains. The basin keeps all the pollen right where it is, sustaining a cloud of immune system-inflaming elements right outside, and inside, my door.

Today I suffer. I smile, I engage, I have a good time. But underneath it all I'm a churning mass of irritated nerve-endings and overproducing glands.

I pray for rain. I don't know any of the dances or chants, so I open my weather app ten times each hour, willing the little cloud icon to produce a lightning bolt, hoping it explodes with pixel-rich rain drops, doing all within my power to summon a pocket-Zeus to bless this place with an antigen-nullifying deluge so that I can be myself again, so that I can remember what it's like to interact with the world without a layer of puffiness between me and my sensory organs.

For those who travel, injuries and sickness are devils you know you'll have to face periodically. They're a series of side-quests you see coming but still must complete, and every time you sniffle or cough, feel a stiffness in your neck or find a cut on your finger, you hope with all your being that it isn't time for a serious, boss-level encounter.

Because although travel is, as much as anything else, about being uncomfortable, a stimulating but arduous dare one accepts again and again, there are certain things that pull you from that oft-perilous but exhilarating reverie and reframe it as something else entirely. Whereas you willingly suffer inconveniences for the sake of the journey, when you're injured, you merely suffer. Whereas once you faced risks in the pursuit of personal growth and new knowledge, when ill you watch your long-term health and happiness evaporate, potentially forevermore.

Cuts and bruises and broken bones and broken hearts and headaches and backaches and sunburns and razor burn and hangovers and bad haircuts and colds and flus and food poisoning and sore muscles and bug bites and dog bites and lizard bites and jellyfish stings are all par for the course when traveling. They're what you signed up for. They're part of the adventure and they leave scars, physical or mental, that you'll show your friends over drinks as you weave them a tale from the safety of a bar in a place with a completely different, better obscured collection of dangers.

The difference between experiencing such discomforts in a familiar environment and experiencing them in one in which you're not fully oriented is that in the latter, something benign could turn malignant in an instant. That cold you caught while staying in the quaint, peaceful little village becomes pneumonia and shit gets real, real fast. That tiny cut you got while hiking in the mountains becomes infected and suddenly you're wondering if you're going to lose a toe, or the whole foot, because you're days from a hospital. That mosquito bite turns out to be a puncture from a poisonous spider, or a kiss from a dengue-carrier. That sore back? A slipped disc that gets worse every day, maybe becoming chronic and haunting you for the rest of your life.

There was a time when mosquito bites demanded my attention, compelling me to scratch near-constantly, my annoyance and inflammation increasing until the itching diminished and my world could return to normal.

Today, having a few bites is normal, and the itchiness easy to ignore. I do, however, face an unconscious concern that this will be the bite that's different. This will be the one that, for some reason or another, comes to dominate my attention. Changes my world, my life, for the worse. Forever.

I scratched my finger while exploring the local rice terraces the other day, and I cleaned the wound the best I was able, then wrapped it up in a Band-Aid. Today I peeked at the wound and worried that its angry red rim might be an indication that the water I used to wash it contained some microbe I didn't know about, or that whatever scratched it contained tetanus or rabies or, I don't know, Rice Terrace Plague, which is probably not a thing, but is maybe a thing.

Think about the food web of a rain forest. A plant soaks up photons from the sun and converts it into energy. That plant is eaten by a series of other creatures, who are themselves devoured by creatures higher up the food chain. This 'chain' is actually an intricate web made from millions of nodes, each one a creature that consumes or is consumed by their neighbors, all of them operate in opposition to or alongside other species, and the whole complex system remains largely in balance much of the time because any factors that would upset the equilibrium eventually die off. Maybe their food disappears from overconsumption, for instance.

We humans are ecosystems, too, and these ecosystems are called microbiomes, biomes for short. A biome is the complete organic ecosystem that makes up a living creature.

Each and every one of us are made up of billions of species of virus and bacteria, fungi and parasites, yeasts and eukaryotes and Archaea. These wee-beasties interact and intersect with our human cells, creating a rich, vibrant, fascinating micro-world which, in macro, is what makes up a complete human. We are the product of these interactions, each one of us the sum of a complex, though tiny, ecosystem.

This is remarkable, and explains quite a lot about how we respond to new environments.

Consider that a person growing up in a large city like New York will be made up of different stuff than someone growing up on a farm in rural Romania.

Riding subways, interacting with manufactured substances like concrete and paint, being exposed to the people from all over the world who converge in urban centers, shedding and spreading aspects of their biome into the environment and as a result sharing part of their biology with others. It's a very specific type of personal-ecosystem that develops in such an environment.

Contrast that with someone who lives and works on a farm, interacting with far fewer people, and even those are primarily people who come from the same environment, who are rich with the same stomach flora and germs, much of their exposure to new microorganisms the result of digging in soil and interacting with animals rather than touching a subway handrail or walking down a crowded street.

Like a rainforest rebuilding and renewing itself, shrugging off those creatures that would throw it out of balance, so too do our biomes struggle to maintain structural parity. We get sick and are exposed to new variables, but the push-pull taking place inside us checks everyone at the door, tries to ensure that the organism looking to join us is a good egg before they're allowed inside. Sometimes these creatures rush right by and have to be kicked out by the bouncer, resulting in sickness as a scuffle takes place inside your gut. Sometimes the creatures are allowed to stay, introduced into your system and adopted as your own, nullifying any negative effects its ilk might stir up in the future. If they play well with your other inner-patrons, they're eventually vouched for. They become a part of you.

When we travel, we expose ourselves to vast swathes of new microbiota, and this means that our inner-bouncers are taxed, overworked, often under-appreciated. Getting plenty of sleep and staying generally healthy helps keep them strong, but maintaining perfect health all the time is impossible, particularly when you find yourself in an environment with wildly unfamiliar local viruses, fungi, and the like. You hope to make micro-friends, just as you hope to get along with the local humans, but you never know whether your biome will agree with theirs, just as you can't be certain that every society will be accepting of your worldview and habits.

Exposing one's biome to new microbiota is similar to exposing oneself to new people and cultures.

Just as with many first encounters between civilizations, there can be strife and conflict upon primary exposure, with each culture struggling to get the upper-hand over the other. Even where there exists a will to live together in harmony, to build something greater than the sum of their individual components, it can be a difficult undertaking. This other culture, their food has such strange flavors, their habits so unknowable, their language has such an odd and disturbing lilt. Clashes of societal norms can result in societal harm, while similar conflicts take place on a biome level: their germs are so foreign, their bacteria such a weird shape, their fungi so unlike our fungi, and so on.

Like societies, though, biomes and ecosystems of all sizes are better off, healthier and more durable, when they contain variety.

A rainforest ecosystem is rugged and resilient only when it's diverse. When there's variety, if some vital component of the web dies off from disease, another can step in and fill that niche. This malleability ensures an ecosystem can recover from even the most debilitating die-off or bio-apocalypse because the system itself reshapes, rescales, and reallocates as necessary.

The opposite is also true. A homogenized ecosystem is far more frail than a diverse one. While there may be surface-level benefits to a system with fewer types of microbiota, if anything goes even a teensy bit wrong in such a system, the entire web is done for. The same can be said for monoculture societies. When a group becomes too homogenized in their beliefs, their genetics, or their worldview, any sudden change in their environment can upend their whole system in a very short span of time. Because everyone has the same strengths and weaknesses, the same philosophical perspectives, the same set of data and interpretations of that data to work from, no oppositional, alternative solutions are present. The biome is rigid and fragile.

Monocultures tend to be more comfortable before the fall, of course, at least for those who are part of the dominant cultural coterie. This calm stems from the lack of conflict in the ranks. Everyone's on the same page, so little push-pull is required. What is there to debate when we're all politically, socially, spiritually, and historically aligned?

Movement requires friction, though, and because there's nothing to push against in a homogenized situation, there's also stagnation. If an entire population's shared susceptibility doesn't lead to a monoculture's downfall, their inability to grow at the same rate as their diverse competitors will.

We increase our own diversity, our own durability, through experience, both intellectual and physical. Our minds grow as we're challenged with ideas beyond those with which we were raised and as we encounter people who have backgrounds dissimilar from our own. As we come to appreciate different views, different interpretations of the same data, different approaches to life and love and happiness, our capacity to experience new things and not just survive, but thrive, grows.

As we expose our bodies to new climates, altitudes, foods, and collections of microbiota, we quite literally change our physical selves, growing as an ecosystem, improving our organic diversity and as a result, our equilibrium. We're not the same people when we return home, in the way we think or on a cellular level.

Not everyone has the same passion or even capacity for growth. We're all different in the ways we think and in how we respond to foreign organisms and environments. But making the effort to expose ourselves to frictions and outside influences allows us to see more clearly what roles we play in the larger ecosystems we're a part of. How we fit in our neighborhoods, our states, our countries, and our planet.

Respecting this balance, in micro and macro, allows us to know ourselves, and to better understand why it's worthwhile to visit unfamiliar places. Which means travel is a worthwhile investment, despite the intense, happiness-shattering allergies we must sometimes suffer through as a result.

SIR COLIN

The girl is underdressed.

Looking at my scorecard, one of the metrics by which I'm judging this girl, and her partner, who is himself not underdressed so much as somewhat underskilled, is 'appropriateness' in respect to both their costumes and their performance. The performance is okay, but not great, and the guy's discomfort seems to be seeping into his rhythm. I should dock them points for the vast amount of skin they're showing to such a conservative crowd.

I don't. I'm cheering for them, a little, internally. I don't know which school this dancing duo is from, but I'm pretty sure it's not the one here in Mayoyao. I can't imagine that kind of outfit making it past the local rounds of the competition and into this inter-school tournament. The people here are open about many things, but consistently demure about others.

My bias will shine through, I think to myself. There was another couple that performed, not the exact same dance but a similar one, another riff on the traditional tango, amped-up with flashy moves, exciting costumes, and what passes for sexuality in a part of the world where that kind of thing isn't acceptable in public. This other couple consisted of a traditionally cute girl and a gender-ambiguous partner. Perhaps a boy going for a David Bowie vibe? Perhaps a girl who's comfortable with a punk-rocker-ish lesbian look? Perhaps someone who's not so cis-gendered, who's bravely displaying a part of her or his self that's something in between; both, but neither?

I gave a few more points than I should have to that couple, because I could tell the audience was against them from the beginning. The people I've met in Mayoyao haven't been at all hateful toward things and people who are different than them in the way some religious folk can be, particularly in smaller towns, but there was a palpable discomfort in the air. Almost as if the pair were breaking some kind of moral principle that was never addressed concretely, never discussed aloud, but which everyone understood to be the polite thing to do. By flaunting something different, something non-standard in terms of sexuality and gender-norms, they had stacked the deck against themselves.

They were underdogs. I wanted them to win as soon as they walked out. Unfortunately, they weren't very good. Not the worst dancers of the competition, but probably the second-worst.

It's remarkable how our peculiarities can set us apart so dramatically and rapidly. Even before we truly recognize each other as humans, as complete people with depth and density, we recognize things about strangers that help us categorize the world. These biases, and sometimes prejudices, color the world around us with tones that guide our actions and opinions.

I'm a big fan of the LGBTQ community, for instance.

Many of my friends are a part this community, and I'm more naturally inclined to have a positive response to its members for that and many other reasons. It's an incredibly rich culture, and is an excellent reminder of how often oppression and segregation and ostracization can shape a society into an increasingly refined version of itself. How something that started out indistinct and nebulous can become incredibly well-defined as a consequence of being squeezed by those who don't quite get it, and who react with fear or violence or harmful negligence.

I think there's something in me, some remembrance of my own outsider status — my own not so horrible and wildly privileged by comparison persecution by those who were better at being 'normal' than I was as a kid — that leads me to feel a kinship with those who are going through the same thing, whether on a simpler or more complex level, whether as a group or as individuals, whether the wall between them and respectable society is tall and well-built, or a short, flimsy piece of material, easily overcome if and when they should choose to test their limits.

What I've come to realize is that most of the same things that made me a bit of an outcast, a geek, a social untouchable when I was younger are the things that allow me to stand out in a positive way, today.

Half my life ago, when I was in my early- to mid-teens, I was bullied to the point that my mother would pick me up from school each day so that I could avoid the harassment and mockery leveled by my peers in the lunchroom, where the debasement was served up most cuttingly.

Today, standing apart, even standing alone sometimes, is one of the traits that has helped me garner an audience, have important conversations, and gather around me a group of people who I respect immensely and feel incredibly grateful to have in my life. In the long-run, standing alone can force a person to become more concentrated and condensed, which over time can give them a sort of social gravity, provided they choose to acknowledge and accept this about themselves.

This same shift occurs in many people after they begin to travel.

A young man from the United States travels to Southeast Asia, for instance, and finds that his differences are celebrated, finds that he's invited to all the parties and flirted with by all the girls. His differences help him rather than restrict him. It's societal geo-arbitrage, a favorable market of human attributes guided by cultural supply and demand. A Western, Caucasian guy is a rarity, a luxury even, in some parts of the world, despite being so common as to be unnoticed where he came from. Similarly, a girl from Latin America may seem appealing and exotic to people in parts of Scandinavia. A transgendered African person may have an advantage in the modeling world anywhere outside their home-continent. Everyone stands out favorably somewhere, in some foreign culture, because of things they inherited naturally; their outstanding features amplified in a positive way because of their rarity.

We didn't earn these advantages, and they certainly aren't always advantageous. The same things that are celebrated by one culture could be stigmatized by another. We've seen this over and over throughout history, as skin color, face shape, height, stature, language, accent, skill set, belief system, familial background, and countless other attributes have been used to sequester and segregate, sexualize and stigmatize people we may know little or nothing else about. Over time, fear turns to fetish, and then back again. Inappropriate becomes proper. Strange becomes the norm. We see this in real-time and we understand how it works in historical context.

And yet the process continues with most of us ignorant of how its invisible hand guides us, certain that we feel the way we feel about people because there is something absolute about them. This person, these people, are a certain way. We know this about these people, despite others feeling absolutely certain about the opposite, and our ancestors having come to another conclusion entirely. Our descendants will, no doubt, feel differently than us, laughing at our quaint ignorance.

Cultural and societal asymmetry can result in some strange situations. Sometimes it allows revered individuals to blend in and play the commoner when away from home. I've known people who are famous and wealthy, near-royalty, in their homeland. When they travel elsewhere, however, beyond the range of their culture's dominance, they're able to shrug off their capes, doff their crowns, and couchsurf like a social nobody. They're able to be just people, reckless and wild, making important, educational mistakes on the periphery of the public eye.

Just as often the opposite occurs. A societally unremarkable person from one culture visits another and is elevated to a higher status. This person is able to meet with kings, glad-hand congressmen, is honored at ceremonies, and is pursued by suitors. In most cases these imports needn't do anything at all to stand out, as their normalcy in one context is what makes them remarkable in another.

I think about this as I watch the next pair of dancers.

Next to me, sitting at a long, elevated table, are respected members of society. Known quantities who have spent their lives adding value and doing good in the region. Educators and entertainers, politicians and celebrities. I'm acutely aware that I'm just a writer who happens to be visiting. Who's enjoying my time in an unfamiliar place, and who, by virtue of showing up, has been elevated somehow. Has been granted unearned honor for providing the value of novelty to a region which appreciates it.

I should mention that I'm uncomfortable with subservience and this is a culture that is quite comfortable with it. Here, 'Yes, Sir's are bandied about with freewheeling abandon, in a manner not even seen in the hipster-sectors of the US where increasingly archaic concepts of status and respectability are experimented with by individuals a few generations too young to have seen the downsides of Downton Abbey-style social systems.

My generation romanticizes Victorian England and the Old West and the US of the 1950s because we appreciate how different the clothing, the habits, and the ways of life seem when compared to our current norms. We admire the top hats, the pocket watches, the well-tailored jackets, the casual day-drinking, the rugged leather boots and belts and saddlebags. We ignore the inconvenient things, like the gender, racial, and religious inequalities. We've never had to experience such things directly, not to their historical extremes. We set aside the 'be a white, straight, middle-class-or-wealthier man, or else' ideology which harshly defined these time periods because, well, their stuff looks cool. Their photographs? So serious. Stern. We want to be stern. We want men to be men, and we don't want to think about how the women suffered as a result as that amplified masculinity. Those are inconvenient thoughts that blemish the cool-factor of the products we fetishize.

There are many places in the world where consumer-grade respect isn't doled out like Mason jars and monocles. Classicism and honoraries aren't trendy and newfangled photocopies of the past here, but rather a state of normalcy, rich with continuity. This is how things are, how they have been, and how they very likely will be for a long time in Mayoyao. When someone calls you 'Sir,' they aren't trying to sell you something, they're just showing respect. Being polite. Continuing a long tradition of good manners.

Actually, everyone, regardless of age, gender, or relative place in the social hierarchy here in Mayoyao calls me some variation of 'Sir Colin.' I consider this a step up from simply 'Sir,' because it makes me feel like I'm being knighted every time I exchange hellos or am served lunch.

I've grown accustomed to this trend, but I'm not quite comfortable with it. In places like Mayoyao, the locals are so friendly that just for showing up you're given the biggest chair, the choicest cut of meat, and the most respectful titles. They dole out deference with the casual grace of frequent application, a complete set of esteemful standards baked into their culture, their traditions, their interactions, their habits.

I know that this is the nature of many groups, but I can't help but pull it apart. Assess it. Attempt to determine if it's okay. Having grown up middle-class in the Midwest, the idea of being elevated above someone else, even just ostensibly, is incredibly disconcerting. There's too much history of forced servitude and oft-obscured memories of Southern aristocracy to make that palatable to any but the most nostalgic of Confederate apologists. Living in an area still coping with the consequences of social stratification makes perceived markers of categorical division quite cringe-worthy.

These stratumic markers are subtle but ever-present. You can see them in how we carry ourselves, in our accents, and on the labels (or lack thereof) emblazoned on our clothing and gadgets. Such symbols, both subtle and overt, help us subconsciously group each other and ourselves based on categories defined by contexts large and small.

When you see someone carrying a purse with a particular logo stitched onto the side, you have some idea of how much the purse cost and resultantly some (preconceived) idea of what kind of person carries such an accessory. Likewise, a person who speaks with a highly enunciated vocabulary might be assumed to have a relatively privileged background.

This is not a new system of passive classist identification. Another honor I received while in Mayoyao was an invitation to dress in traditional garb and take photos at one of the native homes tucked amongst the rice terraces. I was actually a little disconcerted by the offer at first, because it was presented as an opportunity to "wear the traditional local g-string and have photos taken." Never let it be said that I'm not a go-with-the-flow kind of guy. I asked them when and where, while silently questioning their apparently false reputation of social conservatism.

It turned out the traditional 'g-string' is what I would have called a loincloth, and though it showed a lot of leg, nothing untoward was exposed. The loincloth was partnered with a collection of accessories, including a belt, necklace, armbands, and a feathered headdress. I also had a machete and spear, to hunt wild pigs and defend the terraces, should the need arise.

The headdress was ornate, as were the other accouterment, and I realized that the clothing I wore was more than just a gimmicky remembrance of how their regional ancestors dressed: they were also recalling the way in which society was sorted. The types of shells on the belt, the types of feathers on the headdress, these were indicators of rank. They maintain the form of dress and the associated dances and rituals because it helps them remember that they are descended from honorable people and this is how they showed it.

Then and now, each individual identifying characteristic we see in strangers isn't accurate by itself. But when combined with the dozens or hundreds of other little symbols we soak up, they help us decide who is 'our kind of people' and who is not, often without ever having met them. This predisposition can have negative consequences, like racial prejudice or sexism. This is also how political parties become organized and polarized around strange and often conflicting issues.

When you travel, these symbols tend to disappear and change meaning. Sure, there are an increasing number of 'global' tribal signs that are spread through pop culture like music and movies, books and video games, but even these symbols are reinterpreted from culture to culture. I've seen caricatures of laughably over-the-top masculine figures presented for comedic purposes in the US but offered up elsewhere with absolute seriousness. Similarly, a logo or accent or way of living may mean very different things in different places.

As a traveler, I find the rearrangement of these symbols immensely satisfying. I needn't worry about fashion or trend because what's hot in one culture is bound to be passé in another at the exact same time. I'm not tied to any particular set of indicators or logos, which frees me from feeling that I need to be around 'my people' all the time. I don't know who my people are, not knowing what symbols to look for, and so I meet all kinds of human beings from all walks of life, and they challenge my world view and beliefs almost constantly. I'm exposed to a steady stream of unfamiliar ideas from unnamed cultural tribes.

This works in reverse, too. People seldom know what to make of me.

If I traveled to a new city and tried to blend in with the locals, adopting their brands and biases, their hierarchal signals and habits, I might find myself occupying a particular place on their predefined spectrum. Lacking these emblems, I find myself relegated to many different tiers, though usually further up the totem pole than might be warranted. I don't know if this is a precaution on the part of the people doing the assuming, no one wanting to insult someone who could be very important, or if perhaps not fitting in is itself an indicator of being higher-class in many cultures.

Wherever you happen to be sorted within a given society, to be pulled from the safety of your self-presumed status provides the chance to see the world from a different angle for a time. Which is a bit like being famous, if you think about it. Being famous means being set apart from one's peers for some reason. Perhaps a famous person is talented, perhaps they're beautiful, perhaps they're just strange and entertaining. Whatever the specifics, they're perceived to be separate from everyone else. They're revered, sometimes for reasons no one can explain.

I've had the chance to meet some famous people, some who are famous in an larger, more absolute sense, and some who are famous within a specific subset of people. Famous to painters and fans of fine art. Famous to those who enjoy gritty grunge rock. Famous to folks who are always on the internet.

These people do tend to have a certain something going on, though it's hard to tell whether that distinction emerged before they were recognized and labeled 'different,' or after, as a result of that title. I wonder if, in some ways, being a weird member of a group is more beneficial than being set apart from that same group in a prestigious way. Being different, being a bit unconventional, but not being elevated to celebrity status.

Having seen and tasted a little bit of both, I tend to prefer the former, and think being an oddball allows a person more freedom with fewer of the downsides inherent in a more generalized fame.

Then again, there's something to be said for those who stand out spectacularly, embrace their differences, and use the attention they garner as a result to make a positive impact wherever they have influence. You needn't carry a fancy purse or wear an impressive loincloth to change someone's life for the better, or to adjust someone's worldview so that it includes more people than before. All you have to do is show up and be brazenly you.

Though an impressive headdress certainly doesn't hurt.

SHARE OVERSHARE

There are times when I'm accidentally aloof.

I'm told that it can sometimes seem like I hide from view and sequester myself from the world, and as a result come across just a little bit inaccessible. I had someone tell me once that they thought it was a clever marketing gimmick, because the best way to ensure people want you around is to dangle your presence just out of reach.

It's not a tactic. It's a necessity of life, for me. I need time alone. Quite a lot of time, in fact. But fortunately my way of life allows me that time with the minimum amount of accidental insult. If I'm not in the country it's not a slap in the face for the host if I don't show up to a party to which I was invited.

That said, communication is a passion of mine, so finding the proper balance between interacting with the world and extracting myself from it has been a precarious thing. This is not just a concern for folks with pronounced introverted facets, either. Many of us struggle over what level of privacy is appropriate, how to enforce that privacy, and how to balance the need to be alone with the need to be with others.

In a place like Mayoyao, a certain degree of privacy is easy to attain. There are a number of visits from locals per day, of course, but those tend to be brief on days when I'm not going on some kind of tour or participating in a local festivity, and the ladies who bring over my meals are very respectful of my space. That there are few big events going on in a town this size also helps, as there's little in the way of social pressure.

There's also the time zone difference, which works largely in my favor. At night and in the morning I share overlapping wakefulness with people back in the Western Hemisphere, but for most of the day my email inbox and social feeds are blissfully desolate. I'm free to work on what I want without even implied daily deadlines, and I never feel that I'll be interrupted when I get into the zone.

Of course, these same attributes that make this place splendid for isolation also make it somewhat substandard for interaction. In those moments when I want to discuss a topic I'm mulling over with someone who has another point of view, or when I want to share something I've done with people who might care, I'll likely have to wait a while until the time zones realign.

There are moments when this wait feels like years. Decades. Sometimes you just need feedback, opposition, conversation, congratulations. You don't realize how integral these things can be to a well-rounded lifestyle until they're not there and you have to go out and actively find them if you want them.

Technology helps in this respect. Although technology is often blamed for the world's woes, I find that frequently problems are caused by people, not the tools they use. Those issues might be amplified because a person's abilities are augmented by hardware and software, but the tools themselves are not to blame. This in mind, I decided to adjust the way I use my favorite tools to establish a new balance for my new lifestyle.

When I read something I enjoy, I use a platform called Hootsuite to share it with my followers. These posts are automatically scheduled to be shared over time so that I'm not sharing a zillion links at once. I adjusted this system when I arrived in Mayoyao so that it would share some of these recommendations while I'm awake in the Philippines, not just during my usual, US-centric schedule.

I also began to post images on Instagram at night and in the morning, so that folks in the West, but also my new friends in the East, could see what I was up to. I quickly garnered a new group of followers in the area, from Indonesia, China, Japan, and the Philippines itself.

Finally, I decided to give livestreaming a chance. Livestreaming is a video technology that's been around for ages, but which never really caught on in a big way because the quality was pretty bad and the interface unintuitive. Shortly before I arrived in the Philippines, that changed. A few new apps were released that made the process crazy simple, and I chose one called Periscope to start playing with while in Mayoyao.

I was spellbound by how well it worked. I only had a dozen people watching, but they were commenting as I spoke, interacting, and able to provide feedback, ask questions, and tell me where they were watching from. In the past I've been hesitant to get attached to video networks like YouTube because the time commitment required to shoot high-quality videos and then produce them is immense, and often requires a great deal of equipment that's both expensive and hard to travel with. What's more, uploading huge video files simply isn't in the cards for me much of the time because the connection speeds are similar to how they are here in Mayoyao: they exist, but are insufficient for anything too ambitious. In many of the places I live I'm thankful just to have internet connectivity at all, and I'm much happier not having to stress out about massive files failing to upload.

Periscope, however, is relatively bandwidth friendly. I'm able to record almost any time of day, the connection too slow only when a thick fog rolls in or when it's raining heavily. Even when the electricity is out I can stream video, as the mobile internet tower has its own generator separate from the grid that supplies Mayoyao with power.

Perhaps the best thing about Periscope is that it allows me to interact with people only when I want to interact. It's like going on a book tour, but I can show up and leave whenever I want. Because the app notifies people when I go live, if they're around they can join me, and if not they can watch the recorded video any time they like for the next twenty-four hours.

This technology, I realized, could be the silver bullet in my video arsenal. It could finally allow me to show people the things I get to see, live, as I see them.

A few days later I took my small but growing Periscope audience on a nearly two-hour tour of the rice terraces I view every day from above. I pointed out plants and houses and other things I'd already learned about to my audience as I ambled around. A hundred people watched live as I was chased by a dog, was followed by two little girls who kept shouting "Hello! Hello!" while staying just out of sight, and as I walked a balance-beam thin terrace wall, almost falling into rice terraces a few times, barely managing to make my way back home uncovered by mud.

I couldn't stop smiling. I was able to share something new with people, something that I felt so fortunate to enjoy and yet never had the ability to present in a concise and consumable fashion.

Technology gives us vast powers when it comes to sharing, but it also gives us the ability to overproduce. That we're able to so easily generate a glut of calories is part of why so many countries are neck-deep in health crises. Likewise, it's possible to find an app or interface that seems particularly useful and relevant to us and overuse it, leading to excess when what we need is balance.

I don't know what role this app in particular will end up playing in my life. There's a chance it will go the way of so many other technologies in the past, reduced to the category of 'gimmick' by too many people, underutilized and eventually dismissed in favor of more lucrative programmatic pursuits.

But I do know that finding balance in how I interact with others is what allows me to so gleefully live the life that I do. It's what liberates me from expectation and reservation part of the time, and from isolation and omission the rest. Sharing, up to a point, is a useful service valuable to those with whom you share. Oversharing, on the other hand, is a burden on you and on those who find themselves buried by the overwhelming spray of your words or links or face on a live video stream.

Like any balance, it's difficult to know how far is too far, how little too little, until you've touched or at least caught a glimpse of the other side. I'm fortunate in some ways that my desire to have time alone provides me with a built in limiter when it comes to oversharing.

I do worry sometimes that sharing might become too much of a priority, and as a result I may miss out on experiencing the world around me. I worry that I'll view the sunset through the lens of a smartphone rather than through my own eyes.

I want to see the world without a filter applied to it. I want to experience the tastes and sounds and textures of what's happening around me before they're reduced to bandwidth-friendly files. I've remained disciplined in this regard thus far, opting to take in moments first before I pull out my phone to record them. But will this continue to be the case? If pressure builds from those with whom I share, will I pull out the camera a little bit faster each time, eventually bypassing my own experience of the moment in favor of a superior snapshot or feed?

No.

I mean, I hope not. It's impossible to say for certain, of course, but I enjoy these moments too much, enjoy my life too much to share all of it.

My guess is that regardless of the tools I use, I'll continue to treasure and jealously guard the private moments I have, even missing beautiful shots and interesting video opportunities in favor of enjoying my lifestyle myself, first.

Because if you think about it, if you're going to share something with the world, you need to have a perspective from which to share. You need an opinion. You're the filter. And if you don't filter at all, if you simply pass on what's there, no context added, no bias mixed in, you've ceased to be 'someone who shares' and have become just one more device — a thing controlled by the whims and requests of others.

This attitude may prevent me from getting the most out of the tools I have available, but at least it won't hinder me. It won't hamstring my lifestyle or cripple my effort to see, experience, feel, and remember.

SHOULDS AND ARES

I vividly remember a moment from my high school years in which I was driving home, careening up a hill only to find myself blinded by the sun, which was perched just above the horizon.

My sunglasses didn't help, the overhead blind I pulled down didn't help, and the tint at the top of the windshield didn't help. I was near-blind, driving up a hill, hoping that I wouldn't veer too far into the other lane and cross paths with another driver who was paying less attention than I was.

I thought in that moment, "Someone should really do something about this."

That my automatic response to a problem was that someone else should fix it is embarrassing. That I was complaining about the position of the sun in the sky is ridiculous. Perhaps this mostly speaks to the character of my high school self, but I think it also smacks of something many of us who chanced to grow up in the Developed World can relate to, this idea that we're taken care of, that problems can and will be solved. Frictions will be smoothed over in time.

This isn't how it always works, of course. The running joke in Los Angeles (and I've heard it repeated in other cities, as well), is that there are only three seasons in the city: Summer, Spring, and Construction. I don't think Construction ever fully went away in the years I lived there.

Our problems, our annoyances, our little frictions, will be fixed in time, we're told, but perhaps not now. Perhaps not in any measurable, predictable about of time. That's the promise of such a system.

The perception that problems will be handled at some point is often enough. I think the feeling that responsibility for an issue has been handed off, even if we're handing it off to a lumbering, clunky bureaucracy, is satisfying unto itself. Being blinded by the sun as I drive up a hill isn't something I can easily do anything about myself, and the knowledge that there was no one to complain to about it, to blame for it, was probably what bugged me the most. Had I someone to call, a button on my dashboard to report an inconvenience to the sun customer service hotline, you can bet I would had stabbed at it with an index finger and given a piece of my mind to whatever unfortunate soul happened to be on staff that day, listening to hour after hour of frivolous complaints.

In a place like Mayoyao, locals don't have the privilege of complaining and then walking away. If something is bad enough that it's worth complaining about, it's probably an issue that needs to be handled right now.

Driving into town through the mountains when I first arrived, the locals all pitched in to clear a mudslide that blocked the road. Had they not stepped up with their shovels and beams and bare-hands, we would have been stuck there all night, perhaps for days, rather than the hour or two that it took the small army of helpful locals to dig a path.

The difference I see in such circumstances is between people who place importance on 'should's, and those who are more concerned with 'are's.

Shoulds are things that we think should be done, or done a certain way. Traffic should flow in this way, obey these lights and signs and lines on the road, go at this speed. Even if there's no one else at the intersection, you stop, because that's the way things should operate. It's theoretical idealism put into practice as often as possible.

The latter, the ares, represent a more practical approach to daily life. It's an ideology focusing on how things actually are in the real world, and acting in accordance with that. If there's no one else at the stoplight, why wait? Go on through the intersection. If there's a mound of mud blocking the road, dig your way through. It doesn't matter that there should be someone else who's responsible for that job, because the reality is that they're not here and you are.

A should-based system aims for optimal results in every case. It's the consequence of an immense amount of structure and countless systems. It's also something that doesn't tend to exist until a society has taken care of the bare necessities. You don't have a Director of Mudslide Clearance until you've for Directors for every other issue that comes up more frequently than mud slides. Once established, this system imbues different managers and workers with distinct powers and expectations, which allows them, in a perfect world, to do their jobs more efficiently and effectively than a shovel-wielding militia might manage.

Of course, seldom do things shake out in an ideal manner.

An are-based system is a default that relies on generalists. Everyone knows just enough about just enough that they can perform as part of a mob when need be. Some people have more specialized skills they can add to the mix, too, like when a wheel needs changing or pipe needs cleaning. Under this type of system there are fewer people with absolute responsibility for getting things done, though, so many aspects of society fall into disrepair without anyone realizing it until it's too late. Militias are great for solving obvious problems, but less talented at upkeep and preventing problems before they manifest.

I see a lot of are-based systems in rural areas. Perhaps they're not officially set up that way — they're usually necessary byproducts of a should-based system that doesn't work well — but in practice, the locals take care of things, dragging fallen tree branches from the roads, hauling off deer carcasses, and plowing the snow from each others' driveways when their neighbors would otherwise be stuck. This is a system that works because each person involved is very much aware of the other people in their neighborhood, in their small communities, and as such there's an unspoken reputation system that directs one's actions. The man with the plow may not be thinking specifically about karma and a return on his investment when he clears his neighbors' driveways, but he knows, on some level, that it's something he does as part of a system that will help him out if he needs anything. This is his passive, unregulated payment into that larger pot.

It's interesting to watch what's happening to the world as a result of the technologies we've adopted and because of how widespread and accessible networks built atop those technologies have become.

New York City once had a reputation for being a cold,

heartless place to live. Small town kids were warned that it was a dangerous, bitter place compared to where they'd come from, and though that's still the case in some regards, it's not lacking in community the way that it once was. Rather than neighbors being completely oblivious to each other and residents going years without meeting another soul, the entire, sprawling city has been networked, each person connected to each other person, like nodes in a massive web of Christmas lights.

The result is that, although it's still a large, expensive city, and as such people are a little more tooth and claw about making rent and taking professional vertical leaps, it's also a place where you can meet new friends, step into new networks, and enjoy relative safety. It's a place where neighbors help each other and pay their way into the karmic pot. It works this way, even in such a thronging metropolis, because there's a system in place that allows connections to be made and reputations to stick. If you treat people well, others have more motivation to respond in kind.

So rather than a good deed fluttering away into the dark night, unnoticed and neglected, it remains and grows. Each big city, then, is made up of millions of smaller towns, all overlapping and digitally linking people together based of areas of interests, common traits, the street on which they live, and anything else you might think of.

We're all tied together now, inextricably. This means each of our destinies are impacted, even if just in some small way, by the destinies of our neighbors, our peers. If the snowbanks aren't cleared, many of us suffer in different ways, and though the are-based, practicality-based systems still primarily exist outside the should-based systems, the combination of the two that's enabled by these networks that connect people within larger, should-based cultures, makes both stronger. We have the capacity to act together, immediately and when necessary, while still building larger, better, stronger, more ideal systems over time.

I wonder how this will change the world, as the scope and span of these digital neighborhoods increase. At the moment, a lot of the links we could be making don't strongly bond us because our realities, our lifestyles, are still so different from country to country and culture to culture. But ten years from now? Twenty? When the rewards of the digital generation have truly begun to flower and humanity around the world has access to more equal caches of resources? I look forward to seeing what that looks like. To seeing how we treat each other and respond to each others' presence when I know that a stranger on Twitter might be the one shoveling my driveway, and that at some point I may be called upon to help a stranger from Kazakhstan clear a digital tree branch from their digital back road.

We all have ideas about how the world should be, how things could be better, usually for ourselves and our people. But the definition of who is included under the umbrella of 'our people' is quickly evolving as we become aware of those who are like us across boundaries that we once considered to be opaque; freshly breached thought barriers.

We get closer to that ideal world, or some amalgamation of different ideal worlds, by helping making the present, what actually is, now, as livable, as pleasant, and as wonderful as possible with what we have at hand. Even amateur shovelers can help dig a path through a mudslide, and even amateur human beings can help build something glorious for everyone to enjoy.

COMMON

"What's your favorite country?"

This is a question that means, "Rank the countries you've visited for me." I'm asked some version of this question almost every time I'm interviewed on a podcast, blog, or TV show.

It's a fair question, but an incomplete one. It lacks the context that would help me determine what metric we're using to gauge 'best.' Best weather? Best food? Best thrilling adventures?

Even with those clarifiers it's a somewhat vague question, because 'best,' in this case, is filtered through me and my preferences. My favorite weather is chilly with storms and snow. My favorite living situation is a well-designed little flat in a walkable area with the aforementioned weather, and heaters that allow me to gaze out at the freezing squall with toasty feet. These reasons for this are many: I have fewer allergies in colder climates, I don't get sunburnt in such locales, I feel most creative, more capable of writing and making in general because it feels like something is happening outside of my control, which allows me to feel more alive even when holding still, sitting down, typing at a keyboard.

It's a very specific thing, then, my personal 'best' or 'favorite' in whatever category we happen to be discussing. It's filtered through all of my experiences, my priorities, my biases and prejudices, my lifestyle choices, my explorations and limitations.

There is no 'best' of anything, not in an absolute sense. There are places that have more types of food that I prefer, cuisine that is of a higher caliber by international standards, or fare that is more friendly to my palate, having grown up in the United States and having had the culinary experiences I've had.

But there's no simple answer to questions of bests, or even betters. Each and every stand taken on this subject is loaded with context and subtext and pretext. If a firm position is taken, there's also pretense, because deciding that one's own point of view trumps anyone else's is, well, pretentious.

Bests can differ based on where you're located. The label 'best' for food in a place like New York is predicated on standards ranging from the inspiration for the dish to the atmosphere of the restaurant. Maybe the quality of the service. The portability of said food, it being a pedestrian-centric city. Ranking restaurants in such a place must be a complex undertaking because there's so much to consider, and many of these properties are difficult to compare to one another in a sound fashion.

In a place like Mayoyao there are other standards to consider. This is a place without restaurants: there are a few little shops with tables, where the owner can whip up a simple dish and serve it to customers, but I've never seen any menus. These are locals cooking for other locals. The curriculum for 'best' in such a place, then, might be better determined by the freshness of the ingredients, the novelty of the dish, and the friendliness of the person preparing the food.

I'm also frequently asked about the equipment I use, the gear I carry. What's the best laptop, the best phone, the best whatever?

Fancy new things are cool. New technologies, new scientific developments. New civic experiments and inventions. These are the things upon which think-pieces are written and about which puff-pieces are broadcast. We love hearing about where things are headed, what sorts of things we'll crave next.

I would argue, though, that it's more often the common, less flashy developments that are most worthy of our attention. It's the process of making things ordinary that truly shakes the world, even if we don't feel such movements as they happen.

Consider smartphones. In Mayoyao, a few people have them, and those who do possess models that would be considered outdated anywhere in the US by a handful of years at least.

But these devices, even the simple, outdated models, have brought about remarkable changes in far-flung places. Entire new industries are possible because of the casual connectivity they allow. Whole social movements have taken place primarily on networks like Facebook and Twitter and Instagram, on blogs and chat-services and over IP-anonymizing VPN services. Governments have been rattled, others have collapsed. Doers of dirty deeds have been identified and punished and a reputation economy has largely replaced the top-down authoritarian voiceboxes that once dominated conversation in nearly every sphere of life.

These changes have happened incrementally and in such tiny

bursts that we barely notice them while they're happening. But they are happening, and they tend to occur once a technology has become accessible by those who once lacked influence or a voice. Seismic shifts occur when new tools are put in the hands of people who never lacked ideas, just the means of making them real.

In the US, Starbucks is boring. It represents a default, base-level of coffee standards. Below Starbucks are the coffees we all suffered through until the late-'90s, those still purveyed at gas stations and as boxes of pre-packaged stir-ins sold in supermarket aisles. Above the mean-line you'll find the smaller, hipper, aficionado-owned cafes that offer specialized brews. Their beans are roasted just so, then crushed with intent, then brewed with remarkable and expensive languidity. Right in the middle, though, is the forest green mermaid smiling her welcoming smile.

Over the last few years, Starbucks have appeared in cities around the world. I find them on the beaches of remote islands, in the up-and-coming districts of sprawling cities, in podunk towns that barely have a large enough population for a gas station, much less a decent coffee shop.

But what Starbucks represents, what its appearance in all of these places indicates, is that there is a middle-class somewhere thereabouts. There are people who are capable of paying about $3 USD for a cup of coffee. This is a huge cost increase from the $1 or less they were paying before, and that there's enough expendable income being earned in so many and such diverse areas is an excellent economic data point. That Starbucks has become common means that the floors have been elevated, the lower standards lifted. It means that the quality of life for many has been increased, because more people are capable of attaining the type of everyday luxuries a place like Starbucks offers.

It's a different sort of revolution from, say, that of the microchip several decades ago. When desktop computers became affordable for governments around the world for the first time, there was a shift in power as even the most minuscule organizational body had the number-crunching, data-hoarding capabilities of their larger brethren. Then the same thing happened for businesses, as mom-and-pop shops gained access to powerful tools that had before only been attainable by economic titans. Finally, individuals could afford their own keyboard, mouse, monitor, and terminal.

The steps leading up to this were groundbreaking, but it was this last step that led to the internet as we know it today, and several steps beyond that, we find so much of the economic and social landscape has changed that it would be barely recognizable by someone from a mere twenty years ago. This was not the result of a shiny, powerful new gadget made available to the few: that was the age of room-sized computers. The internet revolution happened when a technology was made common, cheap, and widely available to the people of the world.

Which brings me back to the smartphone. Science fiction author William Gibson famously said, "The future is here already, it's just not evenly distributed." So what happens when it is? The mobile internet revolution is arguably already having an even larger impact than the desktop internet revolution has had on our planet, societies, economies, and global culture. To have a device that fits in one's pocket which gives them supercomputer-levels of data-crunching ability, not to mention access to all of the world's knowledge and an always-on connection to any other person on the planet — that's the stuff of science fiction. To give that same ability to every last human being, all seven or eight billion of them, even those who are living in conditions way below middle-class standards — that's borderline miraculous.

And yet that's what's happening. Yes, the newest, thinnest, lightest, pixel-densest smartphone models get all the glory and attention, but the models that are rugged, cheap, produced in droves, and distributed widely are the ones that are going to propel civilization into its next phase. What's happened thus far is the impact of putting these devices in the pockets of about a third of the planet's population. What happens when the next two-thirds get their hands on them? What will happen when the conversation increases in scope, when the number of minds working on problems triples, when the tools we've long had access to are applied to novel problems and in ways we could never have imagined from our Starbucks-swilling perspectives?

These changes are not just occurring in the world of gadgetry. Think about how far food production and distribution has come as a result of certain technologies and practices becoming commonplace.

There's a healthy living movement happening in the US, which at the moment is largely relegated to the wealthier classes. This is at least partially because the tasty healthy foods cost at least a dollar or two more than their fast-food, preservative-heavy counterparts, though that won't be the case for long. The culture of eating local, eating smaller portions of better food, of focusing on purer, chemical-free produce and meats when possible are habits that have spread like wildfire throughout the country. A mere decade after the modern iteration of this movement was first kindled you can find healthy, delicious foods in even the smallest Midwestern towns.

It's not just Starbucks finding its way into every nook and cranny, it's also a food-cart-inspired biscuit truck and high-end salad vendor, each providing dishes that would have been inaccessible and in some cases undesirable by anyone but the wealthiest of customers until just the last few years.

Slowly but surely the processes, produce, and ideologies that support the healthy food movement are becoming cheaper, more widely available, and more productive due to systemization and optimization. It won't be long until it spreads to all corners of US culture, I'm guessing, because the diffusion of movements into the general population has been occurring faster as technology has allowed us to communicate culture, methods, and ideas at quantum-entangled speeds.

I don't think we'll see fewer high-end gadgets and coffee shops as a result of the commonizing of technologies and ideas and norms. We'll see more. Shiny new things are only available, at first, to those with the resources to invest in them when they're still new and unproven. Culture encourages those with spare resources to partake in these novelties, and that indulgence is part of what leads to the innovations that eventually bring the same to the masses.

But that relationship goes both ways. While it could be argued that the resource-wealthy few help bring the scarce to the planetary population, it's the larger multitude of humanity who develop the new scarce, shiny gadget. It's the common billions who riff on and add to the existing components that lead to these new innovations, ensuring that the wheel keeps spinning, the process keeps repeating.

I have no doubt that people in places like Mayoyao, relatively new to the global conversation but taking to it with a remarkable and respectable gusto, will help innovate the next oh-wow-cool thing for middle-class Americans. And we will buy these things, gushing about the novelty, the cool-factor, how wonderful this new thing is. This technology or food or whatever will be sustained by a small number of people, an edgy sub-group, for a time. It will then diffuse into the greater population, the mechanisms of cost-savings and customer-seeking moving beyond their original targets, opening up the gates for other, larger segments. Eventually, a glossy new version of what was initially ideated will reach those who sparked the innovation in the first place.

I believe the beneficial aspects of this cycle can perpetuate even as economic classes become more murky and ill-defined, and as we all come to have access to a wider variety of inputs, inventions, infrastructures, and ideas. Although more traditional systems strain to increase the divide, to elevate some and push others down, such grabs for power are becoming more visible by the day. This increased visibility is the product of a small but growing network of people around the world wondering what might happen if we made privilege and prosperity as common as Starbucks and smartphones.

SUBSISTENCE

The storms in Mayoyao are slow and romantic. They grind and groan, like some massive weight being pushed over an abrasive surface.

Though they can be intense and violent, dropping a deluge that brings rivers of mud and piles of rocks from higher up the mountains onto the homes and roads below, the storms are not entirely out of place in this environment. There's a perpetual potential threat here, energy held at bay, ready to go kinetic. We'd all be under boulders and earth all the time if it weren't for the natural stickiness of the land and generations of gentle settling.

I lay and listen. As I often do in such moments, I marvel that I have the time, have a lifestyle that allows me to take the time to indulge in something so purposeless as listening to the rain. I never have to hurry, I seldom set alarms. When I do it's for my own purposes, my own personal gain and priorities. When I stress, it's for things that matter on an individual level.

When I move quickly, I do it of my own volition and very purposefully, not because someone else is hurrying me along.

I marvel that I was liberated from that 'American Dream' cultural coil that ensnares so many of us. I'm agog that I get to do this, to relax and explore, to see so many unfamiliar things. I'm fortunate to still be open, to be capable of engaging in the act of awe.

It may have been a close thing. I was committed to that other lifestyle, even dependent on it in a way. I defined myself by my potential to earn within that system, unaware or unwilling to accept that there might be other standards of success. That there might be value in listening to the rain in the mountains of a far-flung town in a country in Southeast Asia. The very concept of such a moment was foreign to me. If I couldn't ascribe a dollar value to it, how could I know if it was worth doing or not? How could I know if it added something to my life?

I had spent my adult life doing currency conversions for every act: this much effort, this much time, this much energy expended, this much suffering ignored, for this much monetary meaning. Strange, then, knowing where I came from, that I'm probably the first person ever to be featured in *Forbes* for not making much money.

The story wasn't that the amount I make per year is minuscule. The titular grab was that I earn relatively little and enjoy life so much. I travel the world, see amazing things, meet all sorts of amazing people, have all of my time to spend however I like. I can listen to the rain for days or sequester myself to write a book until it's done. No one has any ownership of my hours, my days, my months, my years, except me.

The response to such a story is a confused one, particularly amongst some of my entrepreneurial friends. When you're a part of that culture, a clever person dedicated to building something of value, something you believe will make the world a better place, will solve problems which plague humanity, will elevate you to a higher status, that of 'successful entrepreneur,' the yardstick you've been provided is a monetary one. If we're comparing relative success and deciding who has achieved more, you look at the numbers in the bank, the IPO valuation, the crazy amount of cash expended on an obscure hobby or a townhouse in an overpriced city.

We go through the motions, knowing that the path to righteousness and professional consummation lead in a particular direction. Many of us think that we'll retire young, getting that first multi-million dollar victory out of the way early so that we have more options moving forward. The money itself isn't the important part, the opportunities that emerge as a result of having that money are what's of consequence.

Few entrepreneurs I know actually fetishize being wealthy for the sake of having a lot of money. What they truly care about is having the opportunity to hurl themselves headlong into their next project, empowered by the prestige, resources, and reputation that their payday represents. When you bypass that milestone, then, some people don't know how to respond. Most people seem to think I'm able to do what I do because one of my previous projects paid out, a huge chunk of cash providing me the freedom of time that they're still working toward. It's happened that way for so many of us that I can't blame them for assuming.

Others think that perhaps I've given up, retired before achieving the requisite resources for withdrawal. "Writing books, huh? Well that's nice. Sounds like fun. Enjoy that." The unspoken implication there is that I've tapped out. That the game was too much for me, so I've opted for a less treacherous road to something like success, but not success as they understand the word.

The most common response I get, though, is a tilted head and a thoughtful pause. People thinking, huh. I wonder. What if. Allowing themselves to question, if only for a moment, the tenets of the faith to which they've subscribed.

It usually only lasts that moment, though. Either because they truly enjoy the myriad challenges of that lifestyle, or because they know if they allow themselves to go down that mental path, they too will start off-roading. Will find themselves outside of a system in which they flourish and through which they gain respect. They'll be unmeasurable by their own standards.

That's probably the most disorienting thing about my lifestyle for folks who're still involved in the headlong rush for VC money, the relentless pursuit of high valuations, the need to be identified as the new Person Who Does Important Things, a young wunderkind for the masses to be inspired by: I can't be measured by those standards anymore. Not accurately. Because it's obvious to any who look that I'm engaged in many of the activities we all aim for when we're running that race, but I broke the rules by not finishing the way I was supposed to.

I can understand how a person, recognizing this, might be torn between feeling discomfort, pity, confusion, and a little bit of anxiety. Anxiety from thinking, if he did this, and he got what he wanted from beyond the Big Payoff without putting in the requisite time to earn it, maybe I could do the same.

Recognizing that there are options other than the one you've worked so hard to achieve, sacrificed so much for, is a difficult moment. I know this firsthand. It's disorienting, and makes your whole world wobble for a moment because you know how things work and then suddenly, out of nowhere, you kind of don't. You're forced to ask yourself difficult questions, like "Am I doing this for the reasons I think I'm doing it, for the reasons I tell myself in order to make the effort seem worthwhile?"

Another uncomfortable question: If one's goals are suddenly within reach but one doesn't take them, what does it say about one's knowledge of oneself and the truth of those goals?

We're each born owning all of our time. As we grow, we learn to exchange our time for money. This exchange defines our relationship with the economy, with each other, and to a large degree, with ourselves. We work for most of our lives, trying to increase the value of our time, to increase the amount we earn for each second we give up for something other than our own personal use.

All you have to do to regain your time, to take some of it back, perhaps all of it, is give up everything.

You have to tear up the contract you signed before you were experienced enough to understand what you were doing, before you understood that there are alternatives. You have to write a new one. Perhaps a contract with a better conversion rate, perhaps one that doesn't involve giving up any of your time at all. Maybe a contract that doesn't guarantee any returns on the time you do invest, but which allows you to keep as much of it to yourself as you desire.

When people hear about lifestyles that allow the people who live them access to all of their time, or even just most of it, they say, "Oh, that must be nice. Wish I could do that."

The truth is, they can. They could. But they probably won't. Because no one wants to give up what they've worked hard to achieve, even if it's not exactly what they'd hoped for. No one wants to start over, or risk starting over, in the pursuit of results that are anything but guaranteed. No one wants to walk paths that are less certain, less safe, less socially acceptable.

People often say to me, "I know I've got a book in me, I just wish I could find the time to write it."

That may be true. But it's also true that we've all got the same number of hours in a day, and if your hours are being spent elsewhere, on work or family or Netflix, you're showing with your actions what your priorities are. This may be because you haven't taken the time to step back and recognize it, or it could be that you've consciously decided that Netflix is more important than writing. Either way, you've made your choice.

The same is true with your work, with your lifestyle, with the contract you've signed with society about what you get in exchange for your weekdays and effort. We show with our actions what our priorities are. Time unclaimed, time traded for something else, is one's priorities in practice.

No one likes to be thrown off the deep end, not even people who take risks for a living. If the tech-philosophers who write think-pieces about their lifestyle and productivity hacks were ever forced to really consider how they live, why they do the things they do, why they're trying to achieve 'passive incomes,' I bet we'd have a lot of twenty-somethings running around, confused, their startups abandoned, their half-finished apps in programming purgatory. Millions of logo t-shirts would go unprinted, thousands of launch parties would remain unthrown.

I don't believe that this path, the asymmetric path, is the right one for everybody. I do think that the structured, well-lit highway of startup land is more ideal for some people, for those who actually enjoy the adventure of leaping preexisting roadblocks and spending their energy living up to standards set by those who got there before them. A lot of value comes out of that system, and for those who would be lost without the work hard, play hard lifestyle, it could certainly be worse.

The same could be said of the paycheck world, and other well-tread paths. For many people these are the roads of least resistance, and the payoff of questioning where they lead isn't worth the consequences of asking those questions.

But for the rest of us, for those who have goals beyond the daily grind, it's hard to imagine a worse way to spend our energy and effort, a worse way to spend our lives. That's what pulled me from my path, even though I questioned my choice at every turn and almost doubled-back several times, returning to the familiar landscapes and hazards of 'being an entrepreneur.' One of the most difficult and jarring experiences of my adult life was when I realized that it would be more correct to call myself an author than a business owner. Yes, I was running a few small things here and there, and yes, I was writing and publishing like an authorpreneur, but I no longer felt like part of that system, where the ends are far-off-but-known quantities and the cost of entry is nothing short of your youth.

I wasn't part of all that anymore. I was some new thing, and losing my identity required that I reassess what that meant and who I really was. It required that I put a fine point on what my identity actually was, now that no one would decide for me.

Rethinking one thing often leads to rethinking everything. There was a period of time in which I wanted to be rich, for instance. But now I'm more fascinated by what happens to people when they're taken care of. What happens when people have enough money to live, but no more than that?

This is, in some ways, what the breakneck chase from my past was all about. I was scrambling to acquire the resources necessary to no longer have to worry about resources. Then, and only then, could I feel secure in working toward less lucrative goals; things that wouldn't payout like crazy for me or my stockholders. I wanted what was on the other side of all that. To be able to work passionately on things that wouldn't necessarily make me or anyone who invested in me wealthy.

While traveling, I've seen examples of what happens when this goal is achieved, though seldom in exactly the same way.

The people here in Mayoyao, for instance, are not rich, but they are subsisting. That word is often associated with the bad old times, pre-industry, when farming was the dominant lifestyle and we produced only just enough to keep civilization rolling along. Mechanical industry brought us the ability to produce more, allowed each of us to be impressive machines capable of generating far more value per hour than before. We were able to specialize, to wage war. We had to invent marketing to create demand for products because we were producing far more than people needed.

I don't romanticize the past. I think we're far better off now than we were during the pre-industrial age. But I also think that many of these decisions we made early on post-Industrial Revolution have consumed us, and have transformed something that should have liberated us from pointless labors into an excuse to work harder, longer, for more of our lives.

Being capable of producing more per hour didn't free up more of our days, it simply changed the expectation, raised the minimum. We were each expected to produce more so that we could consume more during the little time we had outside of work. This system is, to this day, fueled and supported by the idea that we need a certain amount of things to be happy and must produce even more than that in order to feed that existential need. Propagating this system keeps us scrambling our entire lives, running so fast that we seldom have time to question the underlying assumptions of the system.

The people here in Mayoyao don't have the technological wonders we take for granted in the US and other developed countries. The economy is incredibly simple compared to what you'll find in even the smallest North American town. But the people here have a long-standing tradition of producing enough to feed everybody, and to have enough roofs to go around.

Think about that: everyone is fed, everyone has a home.

What beyond that do we need? Not want, but need?

Here, the requirements to participate in this closed-loop system is often backbreaking labor. They work the same rice terraces that their ancestors have worked for thousands of years. Some new tools and processes have been innovated over that time period, but it's largely the same setup as before, tried and true.

Consider, then, what might be accomplished if we were to focus on those same ends, just food and a roof, using the wondrous technologies and systems that are so widely available in the Developed World. How much would we actually have to work each day to achieve subsistence? If we more steadily rolled out automation, and stopped fixating on creating work for the sake of having people work? If we dropped the old models and agreed that we have the resources to allow everyone the fundamentals, and asked how to optimally achieve those ends?

It's a heady goal, and one that's been unfortunately tangled up in politics. To want everyone to live a decent life is erroneously called Socialism or similar things, and the argument against it is usually reduced to "That's an idea that doesn't fit within my worldview, so no, it must be wrong." Many people, even those who solve problems professionally, stumble into this pit trap. I myself once thought the same, though upon reflection my passionate argument against the idea of bolstering mankind's foundations for everyone was more about me than the species. I was offended that I had worked so hard and that others might benefit because from my labor. Why should they, these nameless, faceless entities with whom I shared a species but maybe little else coast on my energy? My capability? Can't they see that my work, my suffering, is pure? Can't they see that my economic theology is the one true dogma?

It becomes easier to see the cracks in this assertion as you meet more people and see how things work in different places around the world. The established, often enforced imbalances make a feeling of superiority more difficult to honestly maintain. Anyone who's really looking can see that the deck is stacked in favor of some and against others. The proposal to provide the fundamentals for everyone, then, is not about empowering some at others' expense, it's about providing the same platform for everyone. From there, those who want to jump can choose to jump. We each decide how high we go. The only difference is that we'll start out standing on the same, firm surface.

We live in a time, right now, at this very moment in history, in which technology is equal to these ambitions. Sustainable energy production is viable at scale, and automation, even artificial intelligence is powerful enough to put most of us out of work, if not now, very soon. If we can get past this bogeyman, the idea that being out of work is a bad thing rather than a liberating thing, and change our systems and biases to suit this new reality, then perhaps more of us can step back and really look at ourselves, at what we want, at what we hope to achieve, and make decisions based on the genuine assessment of productive possibilities and happiness rather than a perceived philosophical purity based on a system that has proven itself productive but also incredibly destructive.

Perhaps we can allow ourselves to shift toward 'better for all,' rather than continuing to fixate on the idea that anyone who doesn't adhere to our standards of productivity are trash who deserve whatever fate becomes them, even if that fate is made worse by the dogma of more that we've forced upon the world.

Maybe someday we'll all be capable of just enjoying the rain and smiling at the storm, rather than worrying how it might complicate our efforts, how the clouds might stymie our internet signals, how mudslides might slow commercial traffic through the winding and unreliable roads that connect the nodes of civilization who play only small walk-on roles globally, but who persist and even thrive by standards other than those many of us are familiar with.

I wonder who we might be as a globe-spanning species if we could combine the wonders of modern technology, hard-earned systems and production methods, and the pursuit of humanity-wide happiness. How might we be different if we pursued fulfillment of a kind that's more difficult to measure, but more beneficial than an extra digit in our bank accounts?

I sometimes feel the weight of immense possibility, and I wonder if it's a change that I'll live to see. I feel fortunate to have the time to wonder, and sufficient resources to sustain myself, to pay for a roof and food, while asking questions that would be considered by many, even a past version of myself, to be wildly unproductive.

YOU START WALKING

You start walking.

That's what I tell people when they ask how they can learn about a new place. How best to explore a new city, learn its ins and outs, figure out what's cool and what's lame, identify the people they'll want to spend their time with.

This is not a complete answer. Few answers are.

But walking is a good place to begin. You find a place to set your bag, if possible, or sling it over your shoulder and hope to whatever god or gods you prefer that you packed only the essentials, and of those nothing too hefty.

Look around. What stands out? Signs, buildings, parks, trees, food carts. Find things that will remain stationary. Cars or people are not reliable landmarks.

Scrawl a map in your mind as you move. Allow yourself to keep tabs on your turns, on other landmarks. Ask yourself periodically, How would I get home from here? Home in this case being the place you set your bag, or perhaps just the place you started walking, a place to which you endeavor to return. Trace the route backwards, guess at how you might take another route to get to the same place, a more direct path, or one more meandering. Get creative, refer to that map in your brain. Do this every few minutes, every time you reach a new intersection, every time you establish a new landmark. Here's a very strange building, you might think to yourself. How might I get home from here and return to explore the weird building's innards, tomorrow?

Challenge yourself to be alert, like the on-screen version of a spy. Note strangers' expressions, their body language. Keep tabs on non-human signals as to the relative safety of the area in which you're walking. Broken windows, excessive non-artsy graffiti, uncollected trash, derelict buildings and automobiles: these are indicators that perhaps you're wandering into a less savory part of town.

Watch the people, as well. Are there parents with babies? Young professionals wearing expensive headphones? Businesses catering to spendy clientele? People sitting on their front porches, not afraid to be outside, to mingle, to be curious about strangers? You're probably fine. Honestly, you're probably fine, regardless. Many places that should be dangerous based on Hollywood stereotypes are actually not bad, and many places that wear the veneer of safety are actually hotspots for crime. Be aware, don't go flashing status symbols, be friendly and polite and don't make trouble, and you'll probably be fine. You're just walking through in any case.

If you find yourself in a new culture, unsure of anything, unsure of even the basics of human interaction and economic infrastructure, find something familiar and explore a little.

A grocery store is a good example. Grocery stores operate in almost exactly the same way anywhere on the planet you might go. There are products available for sale, you can purchase these products from someone there in the store. The people in the store are monetarily incentivized to ensure that you know what's going on, or at least know enough to participate in the exchange.

Notice how much things cost and wonder what that might mean. A city selling teeth whitening mouthwash probably houses citizens with more expendable income than a place that only sells the bare basics. A place that sells skin whitening lotions tells you something about the racial prejudices and hierarchies therein.

Watch how other people queue up to pay and what they buy. Mimicry is an underrated skill, particularly when you find yourself far from the familiar. This may mean going through the motions when paying for a candy bar at the grocery store, and it may mean watching to see when other people cross the street, over time learning to see what they see, watch for the things that they watch for. Maybe they have no signs to indicate moments of safe crossing, but the movement of the cars carries enough information to tell you when it's safe to step into the street. Maybe there's a different sort of sign you would never have recognized as such had you not paid such close attention.

There are places where this advice isn't quite so practical. Living in Kolkata, for instance, I was renting a place on the outskirts of town and had to take a cab if I wanted to get anywhere. Twenty minutes later, on a low-traffic day, I'd find myself in a walkable wonderland, full of things to interpret and people to watch. Had I never made that trip, however, I would have been relegated to the very small parcel of land across which there were paths and roads not dominated by vehicles. My perception of what Kolkata is, the incredible variety of people and ideas, would never have grown and I never would have known the difference. I would have remained completely ignorant to the scope of my ignorance.

This is an important point to make. No matter how we strive to know, to understand, to mimic until we fit in, there will always be more we don't see. There's no town so small that an outsider, or even a born and bred local, can fully grok it all. These sprawling organisms we call cities, and even larger ecosystems we call countries, contain immense and innumerable levels of complexity. That unknowability is what frustrates some, encouraging them to keep it simple and take the familiar route when it's offered, while entrancing others, those who see untread trails as exciting adventures rather than vexing deviations.

Mayoyao has been an interesting home because it contains few roads, but all of them winding and interminable, concealed in places by jungle, exploded in others by dynamite as the locals prepare the space for a new, well-paved beginning. These roads all end in the same way, at one of the two mountainside thoroughfares that carry the itinerant ambler to the next town over, then the next and the next. Eventually you reach a larger city, though those are sufficiently far away that the only practical places to roam, to walk, to explore, are the smaller, oft-overgrown paths that snake through the rice terraces, the native houses, the waterfalls and stone hewn stairways up the sides of cliffs to homes and butchering sheds and tiny schools and churches and everything else a community needs, in miniature.

I wonder, as I wander these now-familiar pathways and roads, what sort of place my next home might be. When I arrive in Boracay, will I find myself isolated, as here in Mayoyao? Is it the type of island to which people retreat, seeking shelter from the outside world? Do they pull palm fronds around themselves, cocooned as they process events from their lives before the island?

Or will it be a raucous party island, roads conjoining at places of consumption and superabundance? A place where people retreat, certainly, but not for the silence or the calm. A place where people go to escape the dull, washed-out colors of the real world. A place where everything is neon and every day is St. Patrick's Day, a place where all men are a fraternity and all women are game to play flip-cup.

When I wander those roads, provided that there are roads to wander, what will I find? Something more of myself? Something new, previously undiscovered? What will I learn about other people? About local cultures, local customs? Will they be unfamiliar, born of tightly held tradition, amplified throughout the years by tourism dollars, but still relatively true to their original intent? Or will they be more of what I've seen so many other places, colors and shapes and sounds and tastes carried over from a tradition spread around the world by globalization, that of malls and intoxication and 'have fun and die young' and the shallowest of sales pitches?

I don't know. You can never know, not until you start walking. Not until you explore, feet on proper ground, eyes making contact with other human beings who are acting out their truths while you act out yours. To hear a story about a place is to see the world through another person's bias. You'll be told of the things they found meaningful, will learn the facts that support their worldview, will be introduced to people they were comfortable enough to interact with.

I'm aware of all this as I tell stories. The context of a story matters, as do the thoughts that go with it. To tell a story without interpretation, without a larger discussion and cloud of impressions and possibilities encompassing it, is to tell an incomplete story. It's incomplete regardless, of course, because it's a filtered view of a place, but providing a bigger picture makes it rounder and more substantial, at least. Denser with vitamins. Not as easy to digest, but better for you.

The final few days in Mayoyao are filled with social activities. I agreed to speak to the employees of the nascent tourism office, a group that moved into their new office building just a few days ago. I spoke to them about using social media, how to live-stream tours on Periscope, and how best to attract and (hopefully) retain new followers without degrading the relationship with their audience by using tricks or gimmicks. We all shared a meal and some coffee, there were hugs all around. I assumed it would be the last I saw of many of them because I'd be leaving for Manila the next day. I'd be on my way to my next home.

That night, though, I was surprised by a group of local friends at my front door. They seemed to think I assumed they would come, though to be honest I was exhausted and had been looking forward to a quiet night. I planned to eat dinner, work out, read a little, and go to sleep early. I had to be up and out the door at four the next morning, so conking out almost immediately was not just a pleasant thought, but prudent.

This was not to be. They poured inside, hooked up the karaoke machine, and went at it. Food streamed in, dish after dish. Drinks were distributed and consumed. Food was shoveled into mouths, mine included, but although it was delicious, my eyes were drooping, my energy levels depleted. I was happy to see them, and humbled by their surprise party. That they would throw me a *despedida*, a traditional farewell party reserved for close friends and family, was a huge honor. But a few hours in, I was sitting at the dinner table staring off at nothing. I tried hard to keep a smile on my face because I felt like smiling, but I was drained, all my energy had been spent preparing to leave a home I'd come to love, a group of people who'd been so wonderful to a stranger in their midst, and a lifestyle that was largely isolated, peaceful, and liberating.

I was surrounded by beauty and was exactly as connected to the outside world as I wanted to be. For a writer, it was near ideal. For a traveler, it was a place I needed to leave, because getting too comfortable is one of the few things that can pull me from my energized, upbeat, curious and fulfilled mindset.

Something you learn after you've traveled for a while is that walking will only take you so far. At some point you need to look around, smile at the memories, at everything you learned and experienced in the place you've roamed and come to appreciate from the ground-level, and then hop on a bus to somewhere new. A new set of roads, a new collection of unknowns to chart.

A new home to come to know.

MANILA

SELFISH

It's incredibly embarrassing sometimes, introversion. Which is strange because it's such a personal thing. In a more literal sense than for most personal things, in fact, because introversion is about being alone, with yourself, so that you can think and process and space out and enjoy the silence. It's the desire to be apart for a while, away from society, away from other people, so that you can do whatever you want, speak not at all, move at your own pace, and fulfill your needs and only your needs.

You want to know what introversion feels like?

This is something I've thought long and hard about, have struggled to define, because it's become important that I make the people in my life aware of what's up. That it's not them, it's me, and that when I pull away it's not a response to anything in our relationship, not an indication of judgement about them or anything they've done.

It's painful, almost. It's like everyone else's words become bullets that are shredding your mind. You're trying to think, to mull, to ponder, to be inside your own head. You're struggling to hold on to something that feels vitally important, but can't. Whether this thing you clutch at is actually important or not is somewhat arbitrary, because your attention is pulling inward and the desire to be extracted from the social situation, be it a party or a conversation or even just a quick flurry of exchanged niceties, is overwhelming.

I've had my entire experience in a few cities colored by the presence of a friendly neighbor or housemate who didn't understand this and couldn't be convinced to give me space. A few times I've lived near a gregarious and charismatic individual who would invite me to things and stop by to ask how I was doing ten or twenty times a day. I scrambled to put up a wall, some social barrier that they would understand and respect so that I could just enjoy my time alone. I needed to be able to view my home as a place I went after being out in the world, after socializing and meeting people, a place where I could recharge my batteries and prepare for another excursion into the unknown. These friendly, attentive neighbors made that difficult for me. Made the experience painful at times. I don't think they had any idea how depleting this was for me, because they didn't seem capable of reading my body language, or even hearing and understanding my words when I told them thanks, but please stop knocking at my door.

Which makes sense, if you think about it. Who doesn't want to have attention and care showered upon them? Why should they be looking for such signals in the first place, when they're doing me the service, the honor, of welcoming me so enthusiastically?

Consider that the words used to describe a good, wholesome kid in school are extroverted words. Social, attentive, plays well with others. The vocabulary we use to describe a kid who's not doing so well, who needs work, is full of introverted words: isolated, daydreamer, hasn't made many friends. This isn't a black and white spectrum. Most people are somewhere in the middle, not an extreme except during moments of intense pressure or stress.

I believe things are getting better for folks who require periodic social isolation. I think more people who are typically somewhere on the introvert side have found their voices in this technological future in which we live. It's far easier for me to talk about all this now, for instance, because I'm able to communicate, live a productive life, and maintain and build relationships from the psychological safety of selective solitude. No one owns my time and my physical space but me, and that liberates me to feel more comfortable in extroverted situations: I know I can leave them whenever I choose.

But to many people, seclusion is not okay. It's not socially acceptable to be antisocial. It's not even morally correct, by some standards.

Consider how many social norms are violated by a person who wishes to be apart from their community. What are they up to? What do they have to hide, these human fragments of civilization? Do they hate us? Are they judging us? Do they think they're better than us? These aren't accurate assessments of what's happening, but those who experience few introverted tendencies themselves can be forgiven for thinking them. How could they know otherwise? Society has primed us for constant interconnectivity.

The concepts of introversion and extroversion were developed by Carl Jung, and are not absolute indicators of anything scientific. Like the Myers-Briggs Type Indicator and the Big Five model, they're labeling systems that allow us to broadly understand things that are otherwise difficult to talk about. In this case, the dichotomous labels define people who are fueled by socializing (extroversion) and those who are drained by it (introversion).

These labels are imperfect and do not represent absolutes. Introverts can be quite social and enjoy the company of others, but also tend to need solo recovery time afterward so that they can recharge their social batteries. Extroverts are more likely to have their energy levels sapped by solitude, feeling most robust and happy when engaging with other people on some level.

I consider myself to be somewhere in the middle of this spectrum, often enlivened and charged by my social interactions, but just as often needing isolation and personal space. An approximate equal amount of both is where I thrive, though it teeters further in one direction or another based on what's happening in my life, what I ate for lunch, or for no discernible reason at all.

I have fairly confident control over this balance, but there are times when I feel pretty horrible about it. As I arrive here in Manila, for instance, I'm experiencing a duality of feelings, one of excitement about meeting a group of local readers tomorrow, but also of embarrassment that I let my battery drain so low last night in Mayoyao.

My friends in Mayoyao threw me a *despedida*, a going away party, for which I was grateful. But as soon as they showed up at the door, food and drinks in hand, the early arrivals setting up the karaoke machine, I knew I was in trouble. After a long day of socializing, of long conversations and shared stories, I had planned on a quiet night in and going to sleep early in preparation for my departure the next day. Instead, I found myself sagging against my chair, then leaning against a wall, barely able to function. I was a psychological limp rag, forcing a smile on my face when I remembered to do so, but fully aware that I wasn't fooling anyone.

I didn't want my friends to think I didn't appreciate the party.

I didn't want them to assume I didn't enjoy their company.

I didn't want them to think that I had better things to do than spend time with them, or that I didn't like the food they'd brought, or that I was an antisocial person.

I just couldn't function. My introversion meter was full, and I needed space, time alone, before I could be a fully functioning social creature again.

What a drag.

I spent the morning dozing in a van as we clomped for hours through muddy mountain roads, periodically cracking my eyes to watch the sunrise, then passed the day on a crowded but not uncomfortable bus, passing through tiny town after tiny town, arriving late in the overpacked lanes of Manila, my battery finally recharged. I met my Airbnb host with enthusiasm and am currently looking forward to the online-organized meetup I've got scheduled tomorrow. Laser tag, drinks, and good conversation all sound wonderful.

I'm reminded that full-time travel allows for near-absolute selfishness.

I use the word 'selfish' not as a negative, but as a reality. On the road, traveling solo, anonymous in many places that I go until and unless I choose to make myself known, I'm able to do what I want, when I want. I eat whatever I'm feeling like, and whenever I'm feeling hungry. I go out or stay in, chit-chat or bury my face in a book. I can expose just enough of myself to the world, however much I feel comfortable with at the moment, but no more than that. I never feel compelled to share more than I know I can afford to share.

This is the not case for most people, for folks who have 9-to-5 jobs and families to take care of. We're so committed to social niceties that taking time for oneself, pulling back when you feel the need to pull back, is often seen as rude. It's perceived as being selfish with yourself, when you should be giving of yourself to those who want you.

This is where introverted needs run up against community expectations. To not hang out when someone asks, to not have a drink when you don't feel like drinking or chatting, to not come to the party to which you were invited, to not relish the thought of a family gathering, is wrong. It sometimes seems that the moral of every movie and television show is that other people are the solution to every problem one might face, and they're also the prize you get for solving any problem. The most powerful force in the universe? Friends. Family. Kumbaya.

So what happens when a person pulls back from that prize, from that solution? What happens when other people are in some ways, for the moment, the problem?

It's not okay. It's antisocial. It's perhaps even arrogant, because why would you prefer your own company to that of others if you aren't full of yourself?

Explaining that this isn't the case can be tricky. We do live in an age where gluten intolerance is no longer outright laughed at in polite company, and we understand that there are myriad variations of the standard human model, so most people are willing to accept "I'm kind of introverted" as an excuse as to why you won't be coming to the party. But the use of that excuse comes with its own issues. Perhaps you'll be treated, henceforth, as someone with a disability, and well-meaning friends and family will check with you embarrassingly often to see if you're okay, if everything's alright, if you feel comfortable right now, and if you need anything to let them know. Once again, well-meaning reactions amplifying the issue. A socially comfortable state of mind can be stopped dead by this kind of attention; it makes a person want to retreat.

If this is the case in incredibly open and accepting societies, places where all sorts of self-identifiers and uber-specific labels are the norm, imagine what it's like in cultures where anything deviating from the ultra-normative is met with a scoff and deep disdain or disbelief.

I've lived in places where they don't even believe in allergies, so the concept of introversion is something I typically leave at home. Instead, I simply tell them I'm sick, or that I need to get home and write. Often one of those two things are also the case, because I'm almost always keen to write, which is something most people recognize and respect as a solitary habit.

I see the pity in some people's eyes when I tell them I'm about 50% introverted. I understand it, that not being connected to others 24/7 is perceived as a fate worse than death to some, because what could be better than spending time with your loved ones? I truly do get this sentiment, and even feel it part of the time.

But I also know the pleasure of spending time in my own head. Of joyfully squandering hours just thinking, staring, assessing and reassessing my own ideas and memories while on a bus or long plane ride, on a train or sitting alone at home in a city within a country where no one knows me, not yet. I wonder if those high-scoring extroverts understand this pleasure, and if they could understand it if I tried to explain it. If perhaps it was a flavor their tongues could catch a hint of, but never express fully as sensory information, in the same way I have trouble understanding why someone would want to be engaged with other people all day long.

I like that I live in a time in which I don't have to hide this facet of myself, or pretend it's not real or not a significant part of how I operate and thrive.

I'm glad I've had the chance to spend years coming to terms with it. Looking back, it's influenced my relationships, and at times has caused me to resent people whose only crime was to spend time with me and want to spend even more time with me. Understanding why that is, and how it works, has allowed me to have healthier, more balanced relationships. It has allowed me to set more realistic boundaries and expectations ahead of time, and the positive consequences of this cannot be overstated.

I'm also more fulfilled now that I've been able to embrace both sides of myself, and can use the paired advantages to overcome the disadvantages of each individually.

I can tap into the introverted side to flourish as a writer, and to allow myself to drop into a deep-thinking mode whenever I like. This has given me the gift of higher-quality and better-understood memories, a more thorough grasp of who I am, what I want out of life, what I believe, and a whole lot of time in which to do isolated, time-consuming tasks, like read and write books.

On the flip side, I've been able to spend better, more intense quality time with the people I do choose to have in my life. When I feel a social momentum, I go out and experience as much as possible, surrounding myself with interesting people, investing myself in new relationships, and enjoying the hell out of those I'm already fortunate to have.

I feel stronger for having this balance, and I would feel a little lopsided without one or the other.

This is an in-flux aspect of my life, and there are still cracks in the system. There are moments when it feels like more of a burden than a blessing, more an anchor than wings. There are times when the wrong side flares up at an awkward moment, and suddenly I don't feel like being out on a date anymore, or I need to go out and meet some people rather than sitting at home, lonely, chipping away at a book I want to finish but on which I can't quite focus. But it gets better and better as I accept the limitations and advantages and learn to work with both.

I'm sitting in my room in Manila, smiling as I think about where I've just come from and where I'm going. About the friends I've made and the friends I'll make. About the work I've done, both internal and external, and how both will continue to grow in the future.

I BRIBED A GUY

I left my place in Quezon City with plenty of time to get to the airport. I was aiming for overcautious, actually, because infrastructure varies from place to place and the traffic in Manila has a reputation for being cluttered at best, but usually something closer to insurmountably stagnant.

In some parts of the world, Google Maps fails to fully take into account local conditions. It predicted this trip would take thirty minutes. It took nearly three hours.

I will say this, Uber makes getting around an unfamiliar city far easier than it's ever been before. Negotiating with taxi drivers is one of the most pronounced and memorable frustrations in most Southeast Asian countries, as the drivers tend to be casually corrupt and view foreigners as piggy banks waiting to be cracked open. In Manila, if you seem foreign and try to get a cab, chances are good that the driver will refuse to turn on the meter (though it's their legal obligation to do so), and will instead demand a price for the trip in advance, that price reflecting an amplification of five to ten times the normal fee. There are also a large number of stop-and-grabs in the city, which means the driver takes you down a road where they have associates waiting, and those associates will open the doors and take your stuff, and sometimes even assault you, though generally only if you fight back. In either case, not an ideal situation.

Uber, though, has implemented a system that is better screened against criminals and in which there's little chance for such misconduct. You pay via an app and can watch a map on your phone to make sure you're being taken along the proper route as you're driving. The fees are also incredibly reasonable: the three hour trip to the airport only cost me about $7. The driver was courteous, the car was clean. It's no wonder such services are slowly but certainly running the established players out of business.

Despite the slog through Manila's perpetually under-construction, over-crowded, directionally ambiguous streets, my cautious planning meant that I still arrived with about an hour before my flight. As we pulled up to the departure gates, though, I could see that it wouldn't be nearly enough time.

There was a line snaking its way out the door, winding its way around the block and measuring a solid half-mile in length. When the driver pointed at it, I didn't understand: the milling mass of people didn't seem like a queue to me. It seemed more like a crowd, shuffling around in different directions, but not organized toward any one goal. Certainly it was too vast to be a line one might choose to wait in. And yet, tracking it back toward its origin, the line did stem from a single pair of automatic doors, the automation apparently broken, the portal physically opened and closed by a guard.

After stepping out of the Uber I watched the door for a few

minutes and only saw it open twice: once to let a man through, and then a second time to let that man's luggage through. At this speed, I estimated that I would make it inside the building by sometime mid-2018.

It took me a few minutes just to find the back of the line, and it continued to grow even as I approached. The immensity of the problem was too big to fully fathom in the moment, but I gamely tried to calculate just how early I would have had to arrive to make my flight on time. I flipped around on my phone and tried to find alternate tickets, as I would clearly miss the one I had scheduled.

I was occupied enough by these thoughts that I almost missed the nod and question from the baggage handler who was standing next to me. I wasn't sure he was speaking to me at first, because he wasn't quite looking at me, was more looking past me. He wore the uniform and name tag of a legit baggage handler, though, so I played along. I guessed it could be the lead-in to a scam, as depressingly many interactions tend to be at official places of ingress and egress, but, well, I had the time to burn either way.

"Huh?" I asked. I'm never sure what language the people around me speak, so I often opt for vague, inquisitive sounds, rather than firmer, dialect-specific "What?"s or "Pardon?"s.

"You're flying to where, sir?" he repeated.

"Kalibo."

"Okay sir, yes sir, follow me sir."

He started walking in the opposite direction, away from the front of the line. He tried to take one of my bags as we walked, but I told him it was fine, I've got it. He shrugged and kept walking.

We arrived at another set of double-doors, the automation

here not working, either, the open-close function once more manually operated by rent-a-cops. The baggage handler spoke quietly to one of the guards, and the doors were opened, I was hustled into the building, and the baggage handler said, "Much faster this way, sir."

I was floored. "Yeah, no kidding! Wow."

"Just don't forget Israel." He had stopped moving and looked at me meaningfully as he said it, and I suddenly understood what was happening.

"Ah, got it. Sure, of course." He nodded and kept walking, and I started to plan the details of the bribe.

There are different kinds of bribes, and they involve all different amounts of money, but there's one rule that almost always applies, regardless of the situation: you have to pretend it's not a bribe, and you have to pretend this with everyone involved.

That means when the baggage handler surreptitiously asks you not to forget him, what he's really saying is that he's expecting some kind of payoff, and that payoff should be presented as a tip, for his help. He'll take care of you, if you take care of him, nudge nudge wink wink.

Participate in this dance a few times and you actually breathe a sigh of relief once that expectation has been clearly established. Until that point, the person helping you is nervous because they're concerned they are perhaps being too sneaky and that you might think that they're being helpful with no expectation of reward. This lack of clarity could result in a more forceful demand, or could lead them to put you in situational limbo until you pay the piper. This would obviously be non-ideal.

Much better to play along and plan ahead. Remind yourself

that this is out-of-bounds, and that they are putting themselves at risk by keeping a sideline gig going. So long as you don't do anything that implies you know you're breaking the rules, and so long as they don't tell you outright that they're skipping you ahead and reducing your screening time from hours to minutes, you're both in the clear. That means if they get mean or overly demanding, you can feign ignorance in a way that would imply mutual discovery. You could start looking for a manager, or asking too many clarifying questions, for example. Typically this'll land you on the other side. Your guide may be a little irritated, but everyone will be happy to have escaped with their jobs and wallets intact.

That's still not ideal, though, because it could result in some type of petty revenge from the person who helped you and who wanted the bribe. You can usually avoid discomfort for anyone by planning ahead in the same way you would during a negotiation. In this case, while Israel was chatting with accomplices who were speeding me through the boarding pass line, I pulled a not insultingly small, but not crazy amount of money from my wallet. Just 200 pesos, or about $4 USD. I kept these bills separate from the rest of my cash, in my pocket, outside my wallet. This way, although I didn't know exactly when the handoff would happen, I knew that I could pull the payment out quickly, say something like "This is all I've got on me, thanks so much," and move right along. This is preferable for the recipient as well, because it means you're not fumbling and asking a lot of questions in an obvious way, which could expose them to their superiors.

While waiting for the boarding passes, Israel fake-casually explained that I was lucky to have found him, and that sometimes people are very thankful to skip the lines and will pay him $40, or even $80 to get them through this way. I laugh in a friendly way and tell him I don't have that much, but I am thankful, and will give him what I can. From that point, I was told, I'd be on my own. But I'd skipped past the bulk of the lines, leaving the main security checkpoint as the only hurdle left to clear. I still had forty minutes before my flight departed. I pulled the pre-sequestered cash from my wallet and handed it to Israel as casually as I could, the same way you might tip a bell-hop at a hotel, and thanked him for his help. He pocketed the cash with barely a glance and said, "Of course, sir. Have a good flight, sir."

I exhaled and walked toward the security checkpoint, the line only a few people deep.

I try to work within the system when I can, and frankly have very mixed feelings about bribery.

I was quite likely chosen from all the people in that line because I looked like a foreigner, and foreigners are more likely to have cash to give an enterprising young baggage handler who's established a few relationships with guards and airline employees capable of fast-tracking his few special 'friends.' Maybe he pays them a portion of the bribes, maybe he buys drinks for those who help out, maybe he just asks really nicely and they have no reason not to help out when they can. Whatever the specifics of the scam, I know that it's not a system that favors any but the select few. All of those other people had to wait in that endless line to get where I was able to go in mere minutes for a measly $4.

In some places, bribes are less optional. While living in Kolkata, I was repeatedly asked for bribes by authority figures, and one time was stopped by an armored personnel carrier full of SWAT-armored police. They pulled my taxi over, claiming that I was sitting too close to the girl I was with, was told it was a very serious thing, this indecency, and that they'd need to take me into the station. It would all be very time-consuming and expensive, I was told. Of course, they weren't heartless. I could just pay a fee right there and then, to speed things along and save everybody a lot of trouble. It was probably a better idea, I was told, because otherwise I'd be in big trouble.

Again, no one was calling the bribe a bribe. I knew what he was asking, and he asked in a way that ensured I understood. But if I directly called it out for what it was, who knows what could have happened? In places corrupt enough to allow such exchanges to occur regularly, who's to say how low criminals pushed beyond polite extortion will go? If there aren't sufficient incentives to not bribe or accept bribes, who's to say whether or not a corrupt cop will beat you, or disappear you? The unknowns of non-participation are far more intimidating than the idea that you might be committing a small crime by willfully participating in the lie.

At least this bribe in the Philippines was an opportunity rather than a threat. It was an offer, an upgrade, rather than a demand leveled by thugs. It was more akin, on a much smaller level, to the bribery system in the US, though in my home-country such things are primarily the wheelhouse of corporations and politicians: lobbying has become little more than a formalized system of bribes, but again, it only works because no one involved calls it that.

Being able to afford a bribe didn't make me any more comfortable with it, however. I knew that going along with it was my only shot at making my flight, so in the moment it seemed like the right path to follow. But does supporting such an underground industry make ethical sense? It could be argued that when the public system fails to operate correctly, it justifies the existence of a non-public, black market system underneath the surface. You shouldn't suffer through inadequacy just because a group of people, who themselves don't use the public system everyone else has to suffer through, declares that you must.

That said, the fact that not everyone has access to the same benefits, the same 'positive racism' that caused Israel to choose me from that massive line of hundreds of people, makes me seriously question the efficacy of such an argument. An imbalanced system is an imbalanced system, whether or not it's balanced in my favor. I'm not of the belief that one needs to suffer for their causes, particularly when that suffering won't change a thing. But might there be a way to formalize this informal system? A way to bring its convenience to the masses, or at least more of the masses?

Can you crowdsource black market opportunities? Establish a means of hiring a connected individual to help you through complexity, escort you past guards and lines? If we could create such a market, it would stabilize the bribe-prices, but also open up such options to more people. Anyone with a phone and a spare 200 pesos could partake, and in those cases when the wait is more tolerable than the cost, that horrible line is still there. A line that, if more people are being hand-held through the process, would likely be shorter than before.

I don't know if an 'Uber for bribery' makes sense beyond pure speculation, but it certainly couldn't be worse than how things currently operate. Maybe next time I see Israel, I'll be able to pay him with just a tap of my phone.

BORACAY

FLIP FLOPS

I hate beaches.

Hate is a strong word, I know. I probably don't really hate them.

I am annoyed by beaches. I'm greatly inconvenienced by beaches. They hurt me, isolate me. They change the way I interact with the world in a negative way.

Being pale of complexion, I can stand to be in the open air, fully exposed to the sun, for less time than might seem feasible for someone who's genetic line has survived this long on a planet continuously bathed in sunlight.

I prefer cool, arid climates. My office is in Montana, and I've lived in Iceland three times for extended periods of time because the air, the raspiness of the wind, the segmentation of atmosphere and moisture, they are pleasant in these places.

It might as well be continuously raining in Boracay. The air is supersaturated with moisture, the droplets beading on my skin, on my clothing, on every surface to which they can cling.

Skin is made sticky and hands are made gross. I don't want to touch my laptop, which is a true tragedy for a writer. I want to hold perfectly still and give the barest breath of wind that I can sometimes feel the opportunity to dry me, even just a little. I wait and wait and it doesn't happen. I just get more soaked by unearned sweat.

There is sand in everything, on everything.

I've been here one night, one morning, and all of my belongings are already coated in a fine powder so light you don't know it's there until you try to touch something or move an inch. Then each granule makes its presence known, shredding your skin to ribbons, grinding your nerve endings to pulp. Even the smoothest of surfaces become abrasive. My food is sprinkled with fine white sand, my coffee has a bit stirred in, like jagged crystalline creamer.

Paper becomes sandpaper. Bag becomes sandbag. Colin becomes sad and uncomfortable.

I have a small room here, which is nice. It's the perfect size for me, and although it's just steps from the beach, and although down the alley is a restaurant and bar that also sells iced coffee, about one-third of the space is located outside, in a screened-off patio area containing a table and some chairs, a sink and a fan. The internet router is out there, and the signal doesn't penetrate the wall very well. The wall which, by the way, is the only thing keeping the glorious, life-sustaining air-conditioned coolness trapped and available for my basking pleasure.

It goes without saying that I've discounted the patio area completely. Lost to nature it is, way out there, beyond the AC's influence and, as a result, beyond civilization. If I sit just right on the bed, which is the only piece of sit-on-able furniture in the apartment, the tolerably cool part of the apartment, I can get a little wisp of connectivity, presumably trickling in through the window. It's not much, and it's certainly not anywhere close to fast, but it's something.

Beyond these walls there is an island of the paradise variety. White sand beaches, picture-perfect palm trees, coconuts laying on the ground everywhere, prettily, deliciously. You could just pick one up, hack it open, and drink deeply of the postcard predictability of this place.

This is why I'm here. Inside, mostly, but also here on the island.

I don't enjoy heat, I don't enjoy humidity. I don't enjoy tourist destinations. I'm not even particularly fond of coconuts. But I do appreciate a challenge. To someone else, most other people, I think, this place would be wonderful. Beyond pleasant. An enviable place to live. I know this. I knew this when I rented the apartment and bought the plane ticket for a seat on a little island hopper from Manila to the airport just across the water. Riding the bus, then the boat, then the van to get here, to this little resort away from home, I knew what to expect and I dreaded it.

That dread was what I was after.

Consider that water boils at different rates, depending on your altitude. At sea level, water boils at 100 degrees Celsius. When I was living in Mayoyao, the water would boil at 99 degrees, because the town is located at about 3200 feet above sea level. There are cities in Colorado where water boils at around 94 degrees, due to its higher altitude, and if you're in Quito down in Ecuador, you'll find that your water boils at somewhere around 90 degrees.

The human species has a remarkable ability to find a niche for itself in almost every climate we've encountered on Earth.

True, we're not yet living deep underwater full-time, but we've established long-term bases in Antarctica and on the tallest of mountains. Give us a few more decades and I think we'll have added at least a few deep-sea laboratories to our list of unlikely and uncomfortable home bases.

We adapt, we adjust, we invent and convert. Our species is wildly flexible, and though it may not always seem so, particularly when something as petty as sand and humidity can ruin an honestly quite privileged person's day, we have the ability to reshape our outlook about a place, our perception of our environment, as well as the world around us.

It was my desire to attempt the former: to spend some time in a location that would be heavenly to some, but a stressful, difficult situation for me. A place that I would not be capable of adjusting to my liking, and as such would be forced, for the duration of a month, to adjust myself. Because although it's quite possible to whine at length about such things, about weather that melts me, about sand that invades my most private of crevices, about annoying salespeople and the theme-parkification of a whole island, it's much more productive to look for the good, look for things that can be enjoyed by me, a person with nonstandard environmental preferences, regardless of how repellant the surface may initially seem.

I came here because I knew it would be a difficult place for me to love, but I'm determined to find something to miss when I'm gone. To find something that will allow me to see Boracay as a home, not just a place I happen to be for thirty days.

I begin with habits.

I find that by moving more slowly, the tackiness of my skin is less noticeable and the sweltering heat is tempered by the slight breeze that is just barely there. I also find that mornings are glorious: the humidity isn't quite so bad yet, the sun hasn't surfaced above the ocean, and the sky, tide, and beach are all quite beautiful. It's a type of beauty that's almost cliché because it's been endlessly reproduced in watercolors and Instagram photos, but that doesn't lessen its impact. I decide that I'll wake up early when possible to watch the sunrise, to take in the beach before it's invaded by vacationers and locals selling to those vacationers.

Flip flops. It takes me a day to find a pair I don't mind wearing, but I would still prefer a good pair of wingtips. Flip flops are uncomfortable and usually quite garish. They can be loud, both visually and audibly. On my first day on the island, however, I'm acutely aware of how ridiculous I look walking around in jeans and leather shoes, so I procure a pair for nearly nothing and start wearing swim trunks and carrying around a t-shirt I can slip on when sitting down for indoor meals.

Iced coffee helps with the heat of the day. As the sun comes up, the air thickens and quickly becomes stuffy. Carrying around a perspiring plastic cup of chilly caffeine helps buffer against the worst of the stifling mugginess, though it doesn't do much to help the discomfort I feel walking around with so little clothing.

I will say this, though: if you want to get into shape, live on an island. It's nonsensical to wear anything more than absolutely necessary in a place like this, and as such you're constantly aware of every bodily contour. I stay in pretty good shape, but I'm extra-certain to work out each day here, and I've even added a few more sets of jumping jacks to my routine, just in case, because I know every passerby will be seeing more of me than even I usually see each day.

I'm not an exhibitionist, but putting a little more effort into body-chiseling seems prudent when living on a beach. I'm not a prude, but I typically don't get this naked in public, and if I can't find any aesthetic pleasure in the clothing (I'm more into overcoats than Hawaiian shirts) I may as well ensure that my own body is something I don't mind wearing, unadorned.

I spoke at a conference earlier this year, and although the overarching topic was minimalism, most of the speakers were super-outdoorsy people. These were survivalists and long-term campers. People who forage for berries and nuts, and build their own homes from mud and clay and plants. They all had the telltale rosy cheeks and calloused hands of people who used their bodies in a way that put them in constant contact with the elements. You don't find that kind of tonality in cities, because we're so sheltered, so protected from the environmental factors that would chap and harden us. There are completely different predators and dangers in the wild, completely different libraries of knowledge one must acquire if one is to survive. These people had encyclopedic knowledge of poisonous leaves and how to defecate in the woods, and I realized that although I'd give it my all, I would probably die pretty quickly living as they do. I'm not saying they'd manage as well as I do in a big city ecosystem, but recognizing that there's an environment that's so different, so threatening to your way of life is an eye-opening revelation.

This lifestyle, the island lifestyle, isn't threatening. But it is foreign to me. I'm certain I can find things to enjoy, though. To love, even. I can establish habits and routines, processes and rhythms. I can live here.

But I'm an outsider, for certain. The people here thrive on this, love the heat and the sand and the lack of clothing. They don't mind the kitschy print shirts and loud flip-flopping of everyone's footwear. This is their dream environment, a place they've gone far out of their way to visit. This is where they want to be.

I will not rain on that parade. I will not scoff or scowl at this place, despite the comparative difficulty I'll have establishing myself here, of finding some scrap of enjoyment to cling to. That this is not my preferred environment is no reason to throw in the (beach) towel and suffer through a month's worth of uncomfortable routine. It's important to be capable of finding joy in whatever life brings, and whatever you bring into your life. I will practice that skill here, though perhaps at a higher level of difficulty than normal.

I like nature. I enjoy being nature adjacent, having access to it for a time. Here in Boracay, I will be exposed to nature rather than it being exposed to me.

I will don my trunks and flip flops, doff any scowl that creeps up my face, procure an iced coffee, and make a go at this place. This lifestyle.

I will endure this island paradise.

WHAT WE BUY

Here on the beachwalk of Boracay, there are no seagulls, and there are precious few crabs. Instead, the local food web is dominated by the street hawkers, muttering or shouting what they must think are appealing keywords at you, like elements on a flip flop-wearing website, inundating the ecosystem with algorithmically generated blog posts and excessive hashtags, doing their best to game a system they don't fully understand.

They say things like "My friend, my friend," and "Brother, look here," and "Yes, sir, this way." Many of them are working from the same script, reciting a list of words one after another, pulling out more when the first fails to capture your attention. "Jet ski? Boat around island? Paddle board?" Some opt for a simpler tact, stepping in front of you, holding the exact same service menu as a quarter of the people you've seen in the past ten minutes, saying, "Massage? Massage? Massage?"

Like incantations these words are repeated, and when they don't work, when the tourists flow right past them as if they're particularly annoying rocks in a stream, the salespeople try again, like practitioners of some long-dead religion repeating a ritual, certain that this time will be different. Perhaps they're being tested and this is their opportunity to prove their faith.

I remember the first time I encountered this brand of marketing, way back when I was living in Bangkok. There were parts of the city I learned to avoid completely because I couldn't walk a straight line for more than a few seconds before being hassled by someone selling a cheap plastic tchotchke, off-brand tour, or less-than-legal service of some flavor.

I became so fed up by this that at one point I decided to stop being passive and vent my frustration. A kid who was probably in his late teens came up to me, a rack of cheap plastic sunglasses in hand, his inventory identical to that of five other people I could see without turning my head. He said, "Hello there, brother. Where are you from?"

This was the hook. It many cultures, mine included, you smile and converse politely with strangers, even when you know they intend to take you down a path which you hope and plan to avoid. You're stuck, then, either being the ill-mannered jerk who won't interact with a friendly local, or the born-sucker who gets stuck in an endless web of these conversations that only ever lead to them trying to foist upon you, their captive tourist, something from their selection of obviously second-rate merchandise.

I said to him, "I'm from the US, but dude, I'll tell you now, I'm not interested in buying anything."

He scoffed and faked a fair approximation of offense. "Hey, I'm just asking how you're doing, man. Just trying to be friendly, you know?" He still held his small display rack of sunglasses, but left them at his side, not holding them up in my face as would have otherwise been the case by now.

I felt a little embarrassed, though I knew he was side-stepping. "Sorry man, but, well, you know how it is. No real conversations here. Just people trying to sell you stuff."

He said, "Yeah, well, I just wanted to ask where you were from."

"Okay." I nodded and smiled. He smiled back.

It was awkward as hell.

After waiting for a silent beat, I nodded, smiled, and said, "Well, have a nice day."

He looked relieved. "You too." He glanced at his rack of sunglasses, which he started to heft, a reflex, I think, but he didn't push them in my face. After I'd taken a dozen steps, I could hear him behind me, using the same line on someone else, using it as a hook to sell some sunglasses.

It was an interaction that underlined something about the way these types of relationships work. Neither one of us was happy with how we were interacting. He felt the need to be over the top with his pitch because he was selling the exact same thing as a half-dozen other people within eyesight, so the only two value propositions he could offer were 1. happening to be engaged in a conversation with me at the exact moment that I decided, yes, I do need a pair of shitty sunglasses, or 2. guilting me into buying something in response to faux friendliness. He didn't want to talk to me, I didn't want to talk to him, but there we stood, feigning interest in one another, trying to pretend our relationship wasn't entirely predicated on systems that grease the wheels for the exchange of money but not value.

The street vendors are similar here in Boracay, though they're substantially less aggressive. In Thailand they would follow me, seemingly for sport, convinced that if they bugged me enough I would give in out of annoyance or fear or some other unquantifiable variable that was stimulated by repeating the same words over and over at someone they've never met and only value for their currency. I felt as I imagine many women feel every day, walking the streets while pursued by men who are trying to forcefully offer them things they don't want, repeating a series of words that at one point may have meant something to someone, but when used by them as heartless incantations, are thin, hollow, vacant shells of human communication. A forced interaction in which one party forces their presence on the other and demands attention in return.

Here in Boracay, the salespeople aim for the same, but either the culture or the island mellowness that coats everything keeps them from getting too emotionally involved. They'll chant their keyword mantras and sometimes step in front of you, but they won't follow you more than a few steps, won't feign more than the most casual existing relationship, won't harass you as if such harassment is a service they provide, the cost of which is three or four bucks-worth of local currency, a pair of sunglasses your receipt.

This is representative of many types of business, if you think about it. Yes, the marketing is different, but it often amounts to the same thing. Banner ads and pop-ups, TV commercials and flyers tucked under your windshield wiper. They're all annoyances that someone is convinced will help sell more whatevers. Someone, somewhere, legitimately believes that interrupting your favorite TV show with a soft drink ad will improve your perception of that soft drink brand. Someone, somewhere, believes that anyone on the planet likes having their internet browsing interrupted with an obtrusive, content-obscuring pop-up. Someone, somewhere actually believes that traditional marketing, which has all the subtlety of a slap across the face, convinces anyone of anything;

anyone beyond those sorry businesspeople who have been convinced to pay for the ads, the flyers, the pop-ups, that is. These are the people who part with their money, and the rest of us have to sit through the fallout.

And so we see that pattern repeated across all technologies, modern and traditional. Here on the beach I encounter and ignore dozens of walking pop-ups every time I leave my flat.

The best that can be said about interruptive marketing tactics is that they're a tolerable annoyance. Like beachside salesmen, these tactics are something that we'd all prefer to avoid, but are also things that no one, on either side, seems to know how to do without. What would the world look like without ads? Without marketing? Without people trying to convince us we need things we don't already desire? What might that look like?

I've seen three potential versions right here on Boracay.

The first is represented by the expat community living in the resorts and apartment communities strung along the beach on this side of the island. Many of them are British or from Commonwealth countries, though there are Germans and Austrians and a few Americans here and there. Perhaps 90%, are older white guys, perhaps in their 50s or 60s, and many have made manifest that stereotype of moving to Southeast Asia, getting a younger girlfriend or wife, and living a lifestyle of relative luxury.

Part of that luxury, I would argue, is that their needs are covered. They have someone in their life who they love (or at least lust over, though most of them seem to genuinely care about their significant others and families), they're living in an island paradise, the cost of living is extremely low compared to where they came from, and they're able to move at a slower pace without it dinging them socially. Having that as a base level for one's life, one's concerns and acquisitional aspirations naturally atrophy, leading one to enjoy more of what's already there, be more in the moment, and covet far fewer consumables. What could they possibly need that they don't have? What new gadget or brand name whatever would improve the already amazing lifestyle they enjoy?

The second is lived by the locals of places like Boracay, but also, arguably, places like Mayoyao. These people live in remote areas, and as such the luxuries that much of the rest of the world craves are either out of reach economically (because of additional tariffs, transportation costs, etc) or out of reach infrastructurally (what good is a super-fast smartphone if your internet is too slow for it to be smart?). As such, major corporations don't advertise as much in these places, and most of what the locals know about these brands, these things the rest of the world desires, is hearsay or speculation. They know about Apple products, but they don't understand why they would want them, or why they would pay more than the cost of a local house just to get a laptop with that particular logo on it.

The result of this is a situation in which more of what one craves is local and accessible. Money may be tight, certainly, but the basic needs are more likely to be covered. In these sorts of communities you don't tend to see homeless who don't choose to live that way, because it's tight-knit and there's enough to go around. People have a roof over their head and food on the table. Access to luxuries beyond the basics heavily depends on other variables, but there are fewer people dedicating their entire lives, every hour of every day, to changing those variables. When the essentials are present, we're less likely to scramble to reach higher rungs on the economic ladder.

The third is my own personal experience, and one that I've slowly become comfortable with over the course of the last seven years.

Imagine that your necessities are covered by work you've already done. You have some money coming in every month, delivered digitally to your bank account, and that money covers your expenses plus a little more. Imagine, too, that any additional work you do will plump up that monthly sum, slowly but surely increasing the amount of reliable income you've got coming in.

How do you spend your time, given these circumstances?

Some might say, okay, I can pay my rent, time to go back to the office and churn out more money, because I need things that this subsistence income won't afford me.

Some others, including myself it turns out, end up going a different direction. Core necessities covered, I began to recalibrate my lifestyle toward the things I wanted to do, rather than the things I knew would bring in the most dough. Yes, many of these things can still be sold or leveraged for business, but I make decisions based on how I want to spend my time, who I want to spend that time with, and where I want to be each day, rather than fixating on a single, monetary metric.

The result of this shift, for me, is that I covet less and create more. I have all the time in the world to waste or spend however I like, which gives me the opportunity to think about who I am, what I think is important, and how I might best spend my day for maximum personal growth and happiness.

A major weight has been lifted off my shoulders. Pulled from that treadmill of earn, consume, earn, consume, I can create far better work than ever before. I can experience things I likely never would have been able to justify taking the time to experience. I can sleep in, wake up early, spend all my time with friends or hermit myself away in a far off place, outside of anyone else's reach.

I feel enabled. Liberated.

And I wonder how the world might be if more people could experience the same. How might others cope with this shift differently than I have?

There are some who believe a Universal Minimum Income might help us stair-step up to a post-capitalism system. This would mean that every single person makes a certain amount of money each month, no exceptions. Not a lot of money, but enough to pay the bills, pay the rent. Living frugally, concisely, one wouldn't need to work at all, or perhaps would only need to work a part-time job for extra spending cash beyond those basics.

This makes sense to me in a lot of ways, particularly as we move toward a more automated future. Progressively more aspects of our day-to-day are handled by software and robots, and industries that have traditionally employed many human beings will no longer need them within a decade or two. What happens then? A system like the UMI might be a stopgap, allowing the capitalistic system to continue while allowing these newly unemployed individuals the time to learn new skills, figure out who they are, or maybe just sit around and enjoy some down time.

There are a lot of potential problems with this plan, and though there have been some city-scale success stories a few places around the world, it has yet to be tried on a major scale. I've seen good arguments for and against.

I'd love to see something like this happen, even experimentally, because it would allow a greater number of people to experience exactly what I've been talking about. A life in which the necessities are provided, and each of us are free to explore things that may not bear immediate monetary fruit. Free of purposeless button-pushing and the production of goods for the sake of producing goods. Free from dutifully hawking ugly sunglasses at people who don't want them, not because we believe in the product or think we're providing a service to someone who needs it, but because we're required to as cogs in a system that requires perpetual motion, whether or not that motion actually accomplishes anything positive.

I've written and spoken a lot about minimalism over the past seven years, the core of which is that we should focus on what's most vital to us: the things, relationships, work, and activities that bring us the most value. We should, in turn, eschew the superfluous, wean ourselves away from the activities that are wasteful, the relationships that drain us, the possessions that hold us back. It's not about owning very few things, it's about owning exactly the right things to have the greatest possible level of fulfillment and happiness. It's about having exactly what we need to have and not spending our precious time, the only resource we can never get more of, on possessions that bring us little or no value.

I hope that we can all have this advantage someday. Not living impoverished lives, not living lives overladen with wealth which requires everything we have as upkeep, not specifically living as expats or islanders or travel-happy authors. But living with firm foundations under our feet.

Not born with silver spoons in our mouths, but born with stable footing that grants us the free use of our time, however we choose to spend it.

RECOGNIZED

I was recognized today while out walking along the beach, iced coffee in hand, sunglasses on my face, as I stared at nothing and listened to the surf.

They were an incredibly friendly pair, a couple from Austria, out on vacation, both of them young professionals thinking about their lives and the trajectory on which they find themselves. They spend a great deal of time trying to figure out if the choices they've made and will make are the ones they want to be making. If perhaps they're taking the well-tread path because it's easy, not because it leads to anywhere they want to be going. They told me that my blog, and my books, had helped them decide to see some of the world so they could better calibrate their expectations and their actions, so that they'd regret as little as possible and wouldn't wake up one day, aged 60 or 70, looking back and wondering why they'd squandered that exuberance, that health, that virility and immune system. So that they'd be able to say, in defense of whatever life choices they made, "I did this on purpose. I chose this way of life, fully understanding what I'm giving up in exchange."

That's a paraphrase of the conversation, but it covers the gist of what was said. I remember it quite clearly because it was similar to another conversation I had with a 19-year-old about a week ago when he stopped me in Quezon City in Manila, telling me that he'd seen one of my TEDx talks and it inspired him to think along similar lines. A little over a month before that it was the same story, but in a different country. I was walking around in downtown Columbia, Missouri, when a trio of college-aged girls asked if I was Colin Wright, and then two of them told the third my life story. All I could do was thank them for their kind words and enthusiasm, and wish them the best on their life paths, wherever those paths might take them. I also smiled for their selfies.

After almost seven years of doing something for a living, aspects of that profession become rote. Writing a book, at this point in my career, is less a massive undertaking and more a decision about when I should set aside the time I know it will take: when to lay down the scaffolding, when to start laying the initial bricks, who I'll have help me fix all the little plumbing problems and put the finishing touches on the paint job. It's not easy, but it's not unknown, and it's not insurmountable. It's a difficult job that I've done dozens of times, and one that I enjoy. It can feel like slamming my head into a concrete wall, but even that pain is a familiar pain, and one that I know bears fruit once I make it to the other side.

I receive emails from readers each day. The number depends on what I've been up to of late, ranging from maybe a dozen when I've been playing hermit and keeping my head down, eyes focused on introverted goals, up to a few hundred when I've done a big interview or have been more active than usual on social media. In some rare circumstances I'll do a very big interview, or be featured in a prominent magazine or on a TV show, and that number will balloon to a few thousand. Answering these emails is one of the pleasures of my work, partially because through them I learn more about the people who read my words and about their lives, and partially because I know that the right words in the right ears at the right time can make all the difference to someone, maybe to the world. All I'm doing is answering an email from a stranger, I know, but what if I can help someone by offering up an understanding ear or a bit of advice at a vital, fragile moment? That's a little bit of effort on my part delivering extraordinary returns. I know this is the case, not just because I've had people who I've responded to in the past tell me as much, but because this has been the case for me, as well. Throughout my life, people I've looked up to have taken the time to share their words with me at a moment in which I needed to hear those words. And though it was likely a small, habitual act for them, it meant everything to me, and helped me continue to grow.

Meeting someone in person is the same as receiving an email in some respects, but different in others. Yes, in both cases you're learning about a person, answering questions, asking some of your own, and producing a bare-bones relationship. But when you meet in person, there's an implicit difference in the space you and they are occupying.

The best way to explain this is probably in terms of letter writing, phone calls, texting, and email. Over time, and in different places, these different modes of communication have taken on different meanings. Back in the day, letter writing was the only option, so it was pretty much the default means of chit-chat until telegraphy came along. Today, though, letter writing has a more intimate implication. We have so many options, so many ways to touch base, to write words at each other, that taking the time to write them out by hand, fold them up, slip them into an envelope, pay for and apply postage to that envelope, and mail it off has become an antique sort of charming. It takes extra effort, and as such, it implies something more than sending an email or shooting off a text message.

There's a difference between emails and texts, as well. An email is default, generic, easy, free. It's an often impersonal means of reaching out to someone with whom you may or may not be close. Most people's email addresses are widely available, posted somewhere online or given to them by their work. Sending a text message to someone's phone, on the other hand, requires that you know their number. These messages, then, tend to be more personal than email, but less intimate than a handwritten letter.

Social media has changed the dynamic by making many of our conversations public or near-public, moving email a little further toward being intimate, but not quite texting-level intimacy.

Meeting someone in person is located somewhere between a handwritten letter and an email. Yes, it can be an impersonal thing, and yes, it's something that's conceivably available to some random person passing by. But in most cases a person you see in the street doesn't have any hold over you, doesn't provide a compelling reason to stop and chat. Someone who knows of you, knows your work, they provide a reason, and it makes me want to stop and chat. And as a result, the level of closeness is out of whack, because I know nothing about the person I'm interacting with, and yet the atmosphere, the implication, is that there are things known. That we share something, some idea, some view of the world, or maybe just that we both know of the same book (mine).

Now, I'll bet some people can just accept this reality and go about their day. People who are capable of more cleanly segueing from personal time to social time, or those who exist solely in a social space, ready to converse any time, any place.

I'm not one of these people. Though I enjoy meeting my readers when they see me in public, the initial interaction often throws me off like you wouldn't believe. When I'm walking around, I'm soaking up the environment and mentally recording details. I'm thinking about a book I'm writing or projects I'm working on. I'm assessing something that happened earlier in the day, or thinking about something that will happen that night. I am in an introverted space, and though I'm in public, I'm also blissfully anonymous, or at the very least secure in the bubble of transit that whisks us all past one another, each person with their own destination, and as such, their own path through the intangible stuff of which time is made.

The result of this dichotomy is that I'll hear someone shout my name, or they'll step up beside me and ask, "Are you Colin Wright?" Or they'll say something along the lines of, "Do you blog?"

It's taken me a lot of practice to just say, "Yes," when asked these questions. For a long while I would stutter through some convoluted, take-everything-into-consideration answer. What if they're talking about some other Colin Wright? Or some other blogger? Maybe they're mistaking me for someone else. Maybe I misheard them. My confusion would then result in greater conversational confusion, and everything would go to hell pretty much immediately.

These days the struggle is in shifting myself from my introverted space into a more extroverted mindset in a reasonable amount of time. Being able to move from a deep-thinking, processing mentality into something that allows me to observe social niceties and recognize conversational rhythm. It can take me a moment to make that segue, so sometimes, I'm certain, I come across as if I've just woken up at the beginning of a conversation with a reader who's spotted me out in the wild. I wonder, sometimes, if this is a bug or a feature for an author, as people seem to be a little disappointed if those who do creative work for a living seem too normal.

The knowledge that there are potentially people out there in the world who know of you, who know your opinions about things and the words you use to express those opinions, who are perhaps your benefactors in the sense that they've purchased something you've produced, in a way enabling your casual ambling, changes the way you interact with the world. It forces you to keep your guard up a little at all times so that even when in a deep reverie, some part of you is practicing what to say in case someone stops you for a chat, some part of you is wondering how disconnected from your environment you can become before you're too far gone to easily shimmy skyward, breaking the surface in time to seem somewhat normal to someone who has a certain idea of who you might be, and will be translating everything you do through that filter.

It impacts the way that you work. You think a little harder before publishing, wait for a moment before commenting on some topic of the day. How will this reflect upon the larger image people have of you? And is this the first impression you want those who are encountering you now, for the first time, to have?

I can only imagine the mental gymnastics celebrities have to go through when dealing with this kind of thing, particularly if they weren't child stars and came to it later in life. Do you even bother going to the grocery store, knowing that you'll have to keep so many tiny things in mind? Knowing that you could so easily accidentally offend or give the wrong impression? That associating yourself with the wrong brand, or getting captured in an Instagram while walking down the wrong aisle could have manifold implications on your career, your relationships, on your self-perception, on your life?

I've had a few years to tangle with these ideas, now, and though I know they're present, and can stop and point to them in the moment if I need to, they seldom significantly impact anything that I consciously do. I wonder how much they influence my other choices, though, and whether there's a bias that stems from being watched that we're all experiencing to some degree in these, the days of the social network.

Yes, those celebrities in the grocery store have to worry about their promotional gigs and casting opportunities should they be caught holding the wrong brand of cola, but we everyday folk have to worry about the same, though perhaps not on the same scale or necessarily for our careers. Our reputations are indivisible from the media in which we're captured, in the metadata attached to our names and faces and the answers we give to social network profile questions. Will our favorite quote out us as having certain political or philosophical beliefs that become culturally unpopular? Will we get caught in the background of someone's snapshot, be turned into an offensive internet meme and have trouble finding love, forever worried that a potential significant other will recognize us as that person from the internet thing? Will something we say, or paint, or write, or share, or pirate, or consume, or ignore become the single element by which we are judged at some point in the future? And if so, is there any way to dodge that bullet, or is it down to the luck of the crowd, some of us fatally hit, some of us fortunate to be standing behind those who absorbed the damage?

Like it or not, this is the reality in which we live, and we're all coping with the repercussions together. Fortunately, with as many problems as they can potentially cause, these tools also precipitate all sorts of opportunities.

As I've mentioned before, I'm often quite the introvert, and the same social media spaces that can invade our privacy can also give us the chance to interact with the world, and all the people in it, in more customized, comfortable ways.

I find that often I'll arrive in a place like Boracay and to the people around me, who I walk by every day, I am an enigma. They can't sort me out or decide who this quiet, cloistered person is. It's not an intentional thing, but when I prefer to have my space, I make sure I'm set up in such a way that I can do so.

At the same time that I'm considered a mystery to these people within shouting distance, I'm speaking daily with folks from around the world on live video, through brief messages on Twitter, though longer essays on my blog, and through dozens of other platforms that connect me with millions, potentially billions of people from myriad walks of life, geographic locations, and cultural backgrounds.

This is not a conflict of action, this is me focusing on the communication mechanism that allows me to most precisely control my interactions. When I need space, when I need silence, when I need to be in my own head, I can have that. Connecting with people via technology-based interfaces gives me that superpower. I can grow my hair out, shave it all off, experiment with different types of clothing and workout routines, eat out regularly or never leave the house. I can be whomever I want because there's no one to regulate me, to passively or intentionally box me in, to pressure me into becoming an archetype of myself.

In real life, the line is not so clear. People will drop by your home, call you up on the phone, interrupt your thoughts on the street. It's not malicious, but it is interruptive, and most real-world interactions require that you socialize on someone else's terms, on their timeline. A phone call means 'talk to me now, answer the phone.' An email means 'get back to me when you can.' The importance inherent in the difference between these two types of request cannot be overstated when too much socializing drains your energy, your health, your sanity. Being able to more carefully curate my interactions allows me to spend more time interacting, if and when I want, with whomever I want, more frequently and joyfully.

Perhaps more important than whether or not we're recognized is recognizing if and when we're worried about it in the first place. And then using the tools we have available to balance out the downsides.

COME BACK FRAYED

I have a policy about possessions. Several policies, actually, but one of them is that I don't go to extremes to protect my gear. If something I own can't survive my lifestyle within the confines of reasonable precaution, it's better that I know this sooner rather than later. It's better that we get that gadget-death out of the way, allow that sweater to unravel or those jeans to wear through. Better now than after they become critical to a trip, a linchpin pulled at an uncomfortable moment.

Travel frays. Not just our stuff, but us. It pushes us, rubs us against uncomfortable realities, the friction creating gaps in our self-identity, loosening and then tightening our structure over and over and over again.

It's an uncomfortable reality, but it's also the main value proposition of travel. To travel without being exposed to anything new is like watching a film that's a bad ripoff of one you've already seen. Yes, it may be entertaining, and yes, there's a certain pleasure derived from a second viewing of a storyline you know you'll enjoy. But indulging in a familiar plot with familiar characters presented in a customary way seldom leads to learning or self-discovery. There can be joy in rote living, but there probably won't be growth.

The water here in Boracay is made up of shades of blue I've never seen before. Staring out at the ocean I try to count the tones, but they gradate so subtly that I have trouble identifying where a shimmery, crystalline, torquoise-esque green-blue fades into an ice-blue, closer to primary but not as close as the sky, something in the water warping the hues, reshaping them, bending the light in so many ways that accurate description eludes me. The colors, the tones, the tints fade too quickly to be labeled, to be limited by words. They cannot be precisely communicated using the iconography of language.

In Mayoyao, the greens were pure, so many tints and shades, each one individually representing the Platonic ideal 'green' if viewed in isolation. They blended pleasantly, interrupted here and there by browns and other literal earth-tones, mud when there had been rain, fluffy, hazy grays in the sky, sometimes sinking down over the mountains, into the valleys, kissing the mirrored surfaces of the rice terraces, their segmented, faultless faces reflecting the mood of whatever was around them, like a skilled conversationalist in a crowd of emotional networkers. There were rust reds and pebble whites there, opalescent grays and rosy pinks. But here there are just the blues, underlined by the sunblasted beige of the sand.

I fixate on these things because, frankly, I can. Colors jump out at me more now, along with textures and sounds. Smells. Little things I would have dismissed had I encountered them earlier in my life now leap to the forefront of my attention. These things have become priorities because living has become a priority.

About halfway through my time in Mayoyao, I was able to visit the local World War II monument, which is perched atop the tallest scalable mountain in the area, a place where a group of Japanese soldiers had set up artillery to bombard the town during the war.

Supported by US airstrikes, a group of American and Filipino soldiers eventually took back the ridge, and now in the same place where troops of various nationalities fought to hold and take ground there's a pleasant lookout spot, lined with beautiful plants. There's a small gazebo with picnic tables, and a trio of concrete monuments: one with a large plaque, one topped with a small obelisk, and one serving as the foundation for a life-sized statue of a US soldier in full camouflage.

The mountain, a historical landmark, is currently under construction. There's a road being built up to the top, made of smooth concrete and wide enough for two cars abreast. It will be an important monument for the area when complete, but at the moment it's in disarray. The road is partially built, the muddy path up to the top is treacherous. I rode up to the top on the back of a motorbike, nearly falling off several times, having to get up and walk every few minutes lest the bike should get stuck in the knee-deep mud. Going up the mountain was difficult and took time. Going down was much faster, but terrifying.

Things happen to places which later come to define them. Look at any monument, any sacred ground, and you'll know what I'm talking about. These are spaces that come to represent something, that come to be more valuable because of their history, because of the stories people tell about them, because of the spent artillery shells in the churned-up mud and amidst the shattered rocks.

The same can be said of people. The things that happen to

us, the events we live through leave scars both visible and spiritual. Over time, some of these events come to define us, either because others know the stories or because we wear them as banners, as sigils, sometimes as scarlet letters, as self-affixed reminders of past ignoble deeds, perceived or actual.

Over time, we all become artifacts. Representations of a moment and place, of something that happened. Of millions of things that happened, some recalled clearly and some forgotten immediately. They all leave imprints, both vital and mundane.

Recognizing this can lead to a great deal introspection, and internal exploration can be uncomfortable. Disruptive, even.

Some people who take the time to explore who they are and what they want — not the stories they've been telling about themselves, to themselves, because it's convenient socially and suits the image they're trying to portray, but who they actually are and what they truly want — find that they return to their lives with a re-magnetized compass. The direction in which they'd long walked wasn't their North after all. Perhaps they'll need to do some backtracking, explore new territory, eschew the familiar path they'd become comfortable walking in favor something unfamiliar. Something that takes them through sparsely lit, maybe even completely uncharted and uncarved wilderness.

That's scary. Not everyone who faces such a possibility pursues its proffered progression. Not everyone wants to give up the imperfect but comfortable reality they've come to know and which they helped shape. A deviation from what's become normal may not be worth the effort, to some.

It's enough to make one wonder if perhaps one's own scars are better left unremembered, one's depths unexplored. But having these options, seeing these alternative paths, expands our minds. Whether we meander and change is irrelevant. Either way, we grow.

It may be uncomfortable growth. It may be that the wrong combination of expansion and contraction can hurt our very fabric, can unravel us, like a sweater that's washed and dried repeatedly. Perhaps living intentionally will change our shape, our size, our color. Will wash us out or stain us.

Maybe a long-held lifestyle choice will no longer seems to fit, and we'll require something completely new if we're to avoid being naked, lacking all protective layers, exposed to the elements.

I try to see these challenges as points of friction. I think of a steep incline, and at the top is something I desperately want. If my life is too easy, too perfect, too hand-held and guided, the incline will be both steep and smooth. A surface without fiction makes climbing near impossible. It's much easier in such circumstances to just slide back down to where I started.

Difficulties, disasters, pain, disappointment; being challenged, broken, tested, unspooled, rebuilt, disconcerted, and hurt; these things tear pockmarks in one's wall. They're life's craters and grooves, and they give our feet something to grip as we climb. They become handholds and ridges that provide us with the means to pull ourselves higher, cover distance faster, and become stronger as our muscles are tested and rebuilt, our bodies adapting to the strain of upward motion over time.

Travel provides us with uncountable frictions. We're pulled from our comfort zones, thrown into a heap of unfamiliar variables, and told to live. Just live. The energy produced when we struggle, when we grow, gives us the torque we need in order to climb. Seeing these frictions as fuel, as substance to burn so that we might achieve greater heights, means that every discomfort, peril, and concern is valuable. The environmental influences which cause us to change become tools we can use to guide our own evolution and ensure the changes are for the better.

We create our own continuity. We mustn't depend on someone else to construct our frameworks for us. There's no one better than us to build the stairway that will take us where we want to be. We may have to learn some new skills along the way, and we may be forced to adjust our trajectories over time. Sometimes these shifts occur quite dramatically, without warning. But we are the masters of our destinies and direction. We are the most capable, competent, correct people for this particular job. All we have to do is recognize this and accept the responsibility.

Like a duffel bag full of new-bought gadgets, we leave our homes shiny and untarnished. There are no scratches on our skin or chips in our paint. We're fresh, ready to be traded in for replacement models if need be. We're commodities, easily exchanged.

With time and exposure, we become unique. We become artifacts, just like any landmark-bearing mountaintop or spine-cracked, ink-scrawled sketchbook. We become valuable for our wear and tear, not just for our latent features.

The blemishes are stories and dents are laughs. Far from losing value as we weather, we instead become increasingly distinctive, our worth increasing with each passing year as we accumulate experiences, passport stamps, skills and knowledge, idiosyncrasies.

We start out as products of a mass manufacturing process, but over time we become one-of-a-kind luxury objects, attainable only at great expense, and unreproducible at any cost.

Being on the road, traveling regularly, brings with it an exhaustion that is the result of all this customization, of all this tarnishing and discoloration and warping and mending of fractures. It's a weariness shaped by the people you meet and the things you do, and an appreciation for something other than what you've had, and a desire to never leave it again. Pushes and pulls, shoves and seductions.

I don't think I'd be able to do what I do, traveling this way, without occasional downtime. Without periodic bouts of isolation and rest. Not just sleep rest, but an easing of the taut mental muscles that pucker and heave, that are spun tight like barbed wire. I can deal with anything for a time, including comfort and ease. I need to decompress. I need to return to some standard pressure-level and reset my dials.

I think of this process as becoming frayed because it's not a matter of being broken: that's not travel as I know it. Travel doesn't break you any more than working out breaks your muscles. But it does stress you as you grow, just as push-ups stress your sinew. Even if you travel all the time, you come back frayed.

Then you put yourself back together again. You're still you, but you're capable of bearing a little more weight than before.

MISSED CONNECTIONS

Boracay is a weird place to be single.

I'm reminded of this as a server at one of the restaurants near my apartment drops off my food, a napkin, and fresh commentary.

"Why you always here alone? Always here just yourself, with no one else?"

I shrug and smile. She accepts this as an answer, thankfully. I've found that any other response provokes well-meaning but unwelcome match-making attempts. A few days ago I had a similar interaction with a male server, but the question was whether I was in Boracay with anyone else. I told him no, and less than five minutes later a pretty female manager came over to speak to me, to make sure everything was up to par, to find out where I was staying, to ask how long I'd be there. After dinner, a number was written on my receipt. I'm guessing it was hers, but it could have been the server's. Either case would have been flattering, but would also run opposite to what I'm trying to accomplish here in the Philippines.

And what am I trying to accomplish? A good think, mostly. A step back and a reassessment. Some writing, certainly, but the writing is a byproduct of the internal observation. I keep stringent tabs on my state of mind, my habits, my purpose. These are things I allowed to gather cobwebs for a significant chunk of my teens and twenties, and ever since I started paying them mind again, back when I was twenty-four, my entire life and lifestyle have changed for the better. Each day is a step above the last, each and every moment worth treasuring. There are downswings, certainly, but nothing major. Nothing of note. For nearly seven years, life has been truly wonderful, primarily because I started paying attention.

My current additional level of attention, this period of extra-special mind-care, is the result of changes I'm considering, some that I've already experimented with, and some that I can feel coming but don't yet know the shape of. One such change is this trip itself. My model for exploring the Philippines isn't radically different from what I've done before, but there are enough differences in the specifics that I'm curious to see how I respond to it as compared to my usual four-month framework. I want to know how streamlining my flat-finding process impacts my experience of a place. I want to know how living a month in each location is different from four.

The travel itself isn't the only aspect of my life with which I'm fiddling. I've been seriously considering diving into other media spheres, looking at an increasing number of TV-related opportunities, even considered starting my own, customized, non-standard production project, perhaps while waiting for something more mainstream to become concrete, or even instead of the orthodox option.

What about social media? How much should I be investing there, and what benefits will I gain with more effort implemented here, less there, and by adding entirely new platforms into the mix?

I've been writing books for a while, but there are new options available in how they're sold and marketed. Does having a longer pre-sale period help or hinder the first week's numbers? Should I be investing more in my drum-banging when a new book launches, or can I continue to get away with my usual, low-key marketing strategy? If I changed something in this formula, would a good book flop? Would I kill an income stream? Would I put my lifestyle in jeopardy because I cut off a flow of revenue or because I opted into a responsibility that requires me to have interactions that I find to be ethically questionable?

And how about relationships?

The last time I had a conventional relationship was in 2009. It was a good partnership with a wonderful person, and it led me to a period in which I questioned everything and recognized something that I always knew, but was afraid to admit to myself: the standard model isn't for me.

I don't want kids, I don't think the traditional concept of marriage would fulfill me or the type of person I'm into, and I find limitations, particularly those that imply ownership of another person or that limit them in any way to be against my values. In the many years since then I've experimented and rejiggered the formula. What I've settled on since then, a model I've found to be a good fit for me and my type, are 'long-term open relationships.' These allow for the shared growth with another person, but without restrictions that don't jive with my lifestyle and how I want to treat another person.

That said, I often go many months at a time without so much as a date, much less dating anyone. This is sometimes the result of living in a place that isn't conducive to non-standard relationships, but sometimes it's intentional. Sometimes I say, "No, let's just focus on me for a while."

This is one of those moments. Coming off of a recent, wonderful partnership that was a little unexpected, I've been hankering for some me-time, a little bit of psychological distance which allows me to more easily focus on personal growth and my needs rather than sharing my mind-space with someone else who I'm missing, who's presence I crave.

These me moments are grand, because although they can be lonely, they also force me to consider where I want to be, not where I am. When you're with someone else you're in the moment because you both need to be on the same page. When you're alone, you can focus on some future moment, some new place, because there's no one to accidentally leave behind, no one who's buy-in you require in order to make changes in yourself.

My situation stands out like a sore thumb here on the island. Boracay is a place where people honeymoon. It's where you bring a date you want to impress. Even the locals are all paired off: the jovial, primarily ex-military expats and their tiny Filipina wives spend much of their time together, eating and drinking and sitting near spots where they were moments ago eating and drinking. There are couples from Germany and Finland and the States ambling about as well, though they're lost in the deluge of Chinese tourists, who move in packs of ten to forty, their multitude overwhelming all nearby tables, chairs, booths, and footpaths. Even these great swarms of people, with their matching t-shirts and backpacks, tend to be paired off. An odd number in Boracay is an odd thing, indeed.

Relationships are considered by many to be challenging, difficult. To be points of stress in one's life. These downsides are tolerated because the upsides are worth it, of course, but I don't understand the draw of such relationships. Why would you fight to propagate something that isn't helping you get where you want to be, and that isn't allowing you to live the life you desire?

One of the main reasons people don't end toxic relationships, I think, is that they're afraid to be alone. There's a deep-seated fear in many that to be alone is to be a failure, to be lost and rudderless, to be a cast-away from that which once connected them to the wider world. If they don't have their partner, a partner, any partner, they have no plans, no aspirations, no dates to keep. They identify as being one half of a whole, rather than being whole all by themselves.

I prefer to be a complete individual, first, and this is part of why I date very carefully, and actually very seldom. A complete individual has trouble dating anyone except other complete individuals, and this is not something we're encouraged to be. It's a shockingly rare trait.

Groups of people are easier to sort and manage. Pairs of people can have kids, can form families, can be predictable, organizable members of society. It's not some kind of conspiracy that we're encouraged to pair off in this way, it's just practical. Traditional. Things have worked this way for a long time for many different reasons, and as such our whole social infrastructure is based around it.

People who fall outside of this schema, then, can make those who play by the rules a little uncomfortable. Because an odd number is someone with whom you cannot double date. They're also someone who isn't on the same lifestyle track as you: no marriage, no kids, no mortgage. You lack the shared concerns that tend to make for better friendships. To some, you may even seem like a threat, like some kind of potential spouse-stealer. Not good.

These are not things we think about consciously, of course, but they're things that we act upon. Part of what makes the wait staff uncomfortable when I walk in the door is that the smallest table they've got is a two-seater. Even our restaurants interiors are predicated on pairs or larger groups, and an individual is relegated to the bar, where he or she can hopefully find someone they can bring back to a table someday.

I understand the desire to 'settle,' at least in the historical context. Settle as in 'settle down,' I mean, though it can sometimes more clearly resemble 'settling' in the context of silt at the bottom of a lake. The idea of settling down is to find someone with whom you can start a family, enjoy the years you're both fortunate to have, and hopefully find some meaning along the way. Modern technology and society has thrown a stick in those spokes, though. I hear a lot of talk about Millennials, a generation that is often talked down about by Gen Xers and Baby Boomers because they defy much of what these other generations took for granted. Owning homes, having a bunch of kids, two cars in the garage, working for the same company your entire life. These are things that were once reliable aspects of life, but aren't any longer. The Millennials' rejection of these recent traditions in order to avoid going in to immense debt, to cease consuming more than is necessary, and to refocus on doing work that they're passionate about rather than something that will simply pay the bills is confounding to many of their parents and older contemporaries.

But the way Millennials approach relationships can stir up scorn in their older peers. We're a generation that were exposed to the internet at a youngish age, and younger Millennials cannot remember a time in which they were not connected to a significant percentage of the global population via this network.

Think about that for a second. That means this generation is aware of many, many more variables than those who came before them. It means they are aware of different ways of looking at the world and the consequences of their (and their forebears') actions.

While once a person would be exposed to perhaps a few hundred people over the course of their entire life, now each and every person with a smartphone in their pocket and a social network sending them way too many notifications each day is exposed to millions of people. Hundreds of millions. Their reach is godlike compared to members of any other generation before them. So the idea of settling, of taking the best you can find of the people who happen to go to your school, live in your neighborhood, or work in your office seems downright quaint. Why 'settle' for what you can stumble into when you can instead search for someone optimal in a much larger pool of potentials?

Now consider modern healthcare and ask yourself why, when an ever-increasing number of us can expect to live productive lives into our eighties and nineties, we would want to have kids while in our teens and twenties. Why not go out and see the world first? Get educated and figure out who we are before being expected to properly raise and educate a kid of our own?

Hell, the world being what it is today, with global climate change and the other repercussions of overpopulation, why not just skip the kids thing altogether? Why not have dogs, cats, turtles, or a cactus garden instead? Why not be happy with your partner or partners, live a happy life, and leave the having of children to other people?

This is a good question with many answers. There are plenty of excellent reasons to have kids and to go through some of the traditional motions, even if they're edited a bit for relative age and lifestyle priorities.

But there are an increasing number of acceptable, even desirable models for relationships, and many of them having nothing at all to do with raising children and having families. This is due to the aforementioned technologies, an increased international awareness, and the widespread availability of new options worth considering in nearly every vital sector of life.

This potential for change is not something we should look down upon, it's something we should embrace. It's not scary, it's wonderful. It will result in a greater number of happy people enjoying custom-fitted lives, rather than the majority of us trying to squeeze into something clearly sewn for someone else.

I applaud this change, and not only because my own relationship model already deviates from the norm. I applaud it because relationships, like everything else around us, are going to evolve. They always have. Do you think people in the 1950s were dating according to the dearly held traditions of the 1850s? Nope.

Embracing this evolution allows us to bend with the times rather than being bent by the times. It allows us to be part of new movements as they emerge rather than feeling like we're outside of them, watching from a safe distance as life goes by without us.

As I travel, I sometimes feel as if my choices in life have set me apart, have pulled me into another orbit far from the primary motion of the planet. As if by not walking in the footprints of the majority of people who have come before me I've fallen out of some understood lockstep, and as such am no longer part of that larger story being written.

But when I stop and take stock, consider all the variables and opportunities, I know that's not the case. I know we're each dancing our own dance, figuring out our own steps as we go along. Even those who live what seem to be very traditional lifestyles have worked in their own variations, their own bend of the knee, tap of the heel, wink at their partner. Or partners. Or beautiful cactus garden.

There are no wrong steps in this dance, and even if we sometimes feel that we're in the middle of a competition, judged on our mastery of the Charleston or the Tango or the Wife-and-Kids Shuffle, there are plenty of other yardsticks by which we can measure our own, independent growth and progression — whichever dance we might prefer.

STORMWALKER

It's so lovely here when you walk the beach instead of the path. Most days, the sun over Boracay is a visual boombox, so I avoid the beach, keeping instead to the relative safety of the palm tree-lined walkway which hugs the endless stretch of resorts and restaurants, massage therapists and cheap selfie-stick salesmen. Today, though, is different.

Today there's a storm. A hell of a great storm.

There's a super-typhoon up north, whipping its way across the Northeastern portion of Luzon, the larger island that contains both Manila and Mayoyao. The former is Southwestern enough to be fairly well protected and the latter is shielded by the mountains, experiencing a great deal of rain and not much else. Here in Boracay, though, we're getting slapped around by the typhoon's tail.

It's lovely. The beach, usually well-manicured to pristine perfection, so perfect that it ceases to feel realistic, is covered with a tangled assortment of seaweed and coconuts and palm fronds and bits of rubbish blown over from the restaurants. The coastline, usually barricaded by tour boats, is perfectly clear, the vast expanse of ocean available for gazing, for staring, for taking in, breathing in, for the first time since I arrived.

The storm has given me powers I didn't have before. The beach, once far too scorching and inhospitable, like the surface of a distant planet, inhospitable to the exposed, oxygen-breathing bodies of human life, had been terraformed, had become something far friendlier. Survivable. Despite the violence of the wind, tearing away bits of the human-sized flag meant to gauge its strength and direction, hoisting tents from their stakes and improperly secured boats from their moorings, I finally feel at home in my current home. The only welcome I recognize as such in a place like this is a reduction of moisture in the air, an increase in wind velocity, and an excitement in the morning, waking up not knowing what to expect, guessing only that it won't be the same, boring, ostensibly perfect weather that's greeted me every morning since I arrived.

The mountains in the distance are like torn shreds of construction paper pulled from sun-bleached pages, each a little hazier than the one behind it, the details indistinct, the edges only sometimes clear enough to trace. The color of the water has changed. There are a number of impressive and interesting grays present, including a rare and collectable set of purplish, slate-ish, medium-grays that are difficult to find outside of well-weathered, primary-painted plaques of the sort you might adhere to an important boulder near a fort on a highway somewhere near the Rockies. There are still blues if you look hard, but they're so close to violet that it would be difficult to confidently label them anything but 'in-transition navy.'

The fringes of the waves, the bubbles of the surf, stand out in comical contrast to the stern-faced water. The choppiness of the ocean surface gives it the appearance of obsidian formed under violent circumstances, while the foam looks like cake frosting created by toddlers wielding professional kitchen equipment. The waves slink up onto the beach, the tideline varying wildly, sometimes devouring the entirety of the shore all the way up to the resort chairs, and sometimes pulling way back, retreating to such a distance that it's easy to imagine running out into the newly exposed ocean floor, grabbing at sand dollars and mollusk shells, discovering, perhaps, a sunken ship or other such booty. But before a plan can be formed the water surges forward once more, the portion of the beach that it touches becoming a mirrored surface for a full ten seconds after it retreats, as if the planet is blinking two different eyelids, lizard-like, the reflection a third texture thickly outlining the water, separating it from the wet, clumpy, far-easier-to-walk-on-than-usual sand of the beach.

There are kids out here, local kids, collecting stranded crabs and plopping them into plastic cups. The activity is a familiar one: growing up in Missouri we'd capture fireflies, beetles, newts, and other Midwestern creatures so that we could put them in glass jars with a random assortment of twigs, leaves, and other things we imagined to be the height of interior decoration fashion for such creatures. We would, of course, lose interest after maybe an hour of flurried pursuit, imprisonment, furnishing, and then staring wide-eyed at our new pet, desperately hoping it would do something interesting. I don't know if these insects and lizards died in captivity or if they were released by my parents at some point; I don't think my attention span was long enough at the time to ever make it further than that before running off to read a book or play some video game.

These kids are going through the same motions, though

instead of capturing bugs and newts, here it's the crabs that get the bachelor apartment treatment. The kids fill the bottom of a red plastic cup with sea silt, insert a few carefully chosen rocks and shells, and then drop the struggling shellfish into his new home/prison.

I wonder about this need to own things, to possess them. Here I am on this beach, this beautiful place filled with beautiful things, and still the most common activity I see is consumption. People grabbing at things, struggling to own more. Always more.

I do understand the system, and I get that places like this depend on those cash registers remaining restive, but it's all the more difficult to accept this state of being, this default, when I'm in a place where there's so much value to be had in just sitting there. So much beauty to see, so much wind to feel on one's face. There are literally coconuts everywhere you look, littering the ground from the path to the waves, but our interactions, our 'we're having fun' feeling, is triggered by the spending of money. So couples and groups still wander up to the coconut stand, their cheaply made, locally bought, terribly ugly hats pulled low against the wind, as they hand over wads of cash so they can feel like they're alive

The most important consideration we can imagine for these captive newts, these incarcerated crabs, the only need of theirs we consider to be vital enough to take care of, is how their home is decorated. Before food, before even their freedom, we want to make sure they have the right decor in their little prison cups and death jars.

The internet has been finicky, almost completely blacked out, since the storm started a few days ago. I had an antenna all to myself in Mayoyao, but here there's a legion of expats and tourists trying to tap the same WiFi spigot, and the resource itself is receiving precious little signal from the satellites through which it's fed. I keep the notifications on my phone off most of the time, but it can be maddening when you take the time to check your phone, hoping for news from the outside, and all you see is the same old screen, the same old apps, nothing but the physical world around you to keep you company; the umbilical that connects you to the rest of human society snipped clean.

I smile as the wind sandblasts my face and think, it could be worse.

The only notifications here, now, are physical ones.

There's some kind of bite on the skin over my left ribcage, and it itches a little, even now, a week after I first noticed it. Spider bite? Particularly impressive mosquito bite? Not sure, but the flapping of my shirt fabric over the top of it is sending itchy pings my way, directing my awareness with an intensity, a reality, that few tweets could manage. It's still not as annoying, I think, as the barrage of text message, Facebook, Snapchat, and other notifications most people seem to have set to high-alert on their phones. Very often the things that make us feel important, loved, connected, are also the things that stress us the hell out. We have no way of prioritizing one ping over another, and no means of deciding whether that ping should take precedence over, say, staring at an endless expanse of ocean.

My most treasured relationships are those that don't require me to be in touch all the time. My relationships with my family, with best friends, my romantic relationships, all are with people who treasure their own time as much as I treasure mine. These are people who I can connect with and with whom I always have something new to talk about because between now and the last time we spoke, we've each new experiences, learned new things. Phones are clicked off and bug bites are avoided when possible so that we can think clearly for long stretches without having our trains of thought derailed.

It's remarkable how rare this is, and how difficult it is to make this priority clear to those who would prefer to be in constant contact. Many, many times I've had to subtly slide away from conversations because the person on the other end hasn't realized that I have things to do other than be engaged in that one conversation.

We're surrounded by a nimbus of media which defines our online presence in the same way the clothing we wear and way we walk defines our real world presence.

Being capable of managing both is a wonderful skill to have. It allows you to tell the story of 'you' properly. To share with the world that which you think is important and interesting while avoiding potential miscommunications about your ideas, beliefs, associations, and anything else that can easily be misconstrued or misinterpreted.

Just as important, though, is being able to walk away from that telling of stories and juggling of avatars and compiling of clothing combinations so that you can just live. Take the time to set it up, but then to enjoy the benefits of all that effort. Experience things without worrying about how you'll be seen by others. Give yourself permission to just be you, take things in, soak up the atmosphere, feel the wind, and watch the kids play with their poor, death-row crab, because you may not get to do so again.

You can fiddle with the contrast on your profile picture anytime you like, but the conversation you're having with the stranger at the train station in Smolensk? That coconut you found on the ground and figured out to hack open and drink from? That specific combination of storm and beach and absolute contentedness you're experiencing right now, in this moment, in this place you're only just fully appreciating? Those are not things you'll be able to summon up with the tap of your finger during your daily commute. They're not things you can revisit in a clipped, composed, and filtered format.

These are the things that make up your life. What's the point of all that preparation and optimization if you're not going to live the life you've spent so long preparing for?

CORNER PUB

It's impossible not to notice that every single male at this restaurant is a round white dude with an impressive gut, a stretched out and strained graphic t-shirt, and worn-in shorts. They wear flip flops, all of them. They're day-drinking: it's 11am and my coffee is very out of place amongst all the morning beers and aspirational fizzy tonic-and-liquor beverages. Many of the men are sitting next to their tiny Filipina wives and girlfriends.

These men are friendly. Welcoming. I haven't yet felt like an outsider, though I very clearly am. The shared hobby on this island, in this restaurant-with-a-bar and every other of its kind that I've stepped into, involves hanging around inside, then outside, then inside again, staring out the windows, talking to the other men about shipments of this, orders of that, commenting upon the rear-ends of young women as they walk by, and periodically having a meat-heavy meal alongside their alcohol.

I get my coffee here each morning, and the price is always

different depending on who's behind the counter. I can't decide if some of the girls who work the bar are giving me a discount or if there's just no consensus about how much an iced coffee should cost. In those early morning hours there are usually a few men inside drinking a beer, trading war stories. In some cases these are actual stories about war, in others they're pirates' tales about that excellent shipment of eggs they procured that one time, the one they brought to the island and from which they made a hefty profit. If you're like me and tend to allow yourself to get pulled down a rabbit hole when a stranger starts talking at you, you'll hear other sorts of tales.

One man tells me about his adventures in Ghana, providing a bit of background about how his family made it there and what role they played in a revolution that he says no one, anywhere, remembers today.

Another leans in conspiratorially and divulges without provocation that, yes, he's killed men. Many men. And he still could. He's very adamant that he could kill again if he needed to, if he wanted to. His face is so friendly, his smile so wide, the clink of his beer against the plastic cup holding my iced coffee so earnest, I can't help but smile back despite the implied threat in the incredibly bizarre, context-free disclosure.

There's a lot of tradition in this sort of space. The corner pub is a itself a cornerstone of British society, and has filtered out into other Commonwealth cultures. Most of the men in these bars, restaurants, combination bar/restaurants, are maintaining that tradition whether they were brought up with it or not. This place, which is conveniently located at the corner of the beachside walkway and an alley that leads inland toward town, is their home beyond their actual home. And in many ways this pub is probably even more important than the place where they lay their heads at night. Because here, in this space, is where they're reminded that they're men. This is where the young girls on the wait staff flirt casually and brush hands across shoulders before submitting an order. This is where the front of the building is opened up toward the ocean, providing an unobstructed view of both water and passersby, so that appreciative nods can be exchanged with other men when a particularly aesthetically pleasing young lady walks by.

They're seldom not there, these men at their corner pubs. And I can't really blame them. To them and to a significant chunk of their generation, this place is their internet. This is where they swap stories and glean knowledge. This is where they catch up with their friends and hear about the news. This is where they're exposed to ideas, people, possibilities, and where they can be open to such things comfortably, without having to muss up the predictable lifestyle they've carved out for themselves betwixt the sand and beach chairs and hubbub of transient tourists.

Here's a strange admission: other guys try to 'bro out' with me a lot, and I'm not really into it.

In this context, broing out refers to the desire of guys to chat about 'guy things' with other guys. So it primarily involves talking about sports and fighting and woman's bodies.

I'm not even kidding, these are the main topics of conversation that guys bring up with other guys, and not just on TV. I think it must be some kind of masculine defense mechanism, a default that was agreed upon at some point, by the bros of old. I picture one old caveman advising another, younger caveman, "If you don't know anything else about a person, or if you're concerned that, perhaps, this other person may be questioning your manhood, hit them with a football stat or tell them how much you like the ladies. That'll show them how strong and impressive and totally heterosexual you are." Then they clink stone-mugs full of, I don't know, mammoth beer.

Unfortunately, guys are very easily threatened by one another. It's partially a biological thing, and that hair-trigger defensiveness was probably useful way back in the day when out hunting judgmental antelope who might question one's masculinity, but it's also very much a cultural thing.

The evolution of guy-culture is something I've been cringe-watching with great interest, because many of the cultures I'm adjacent to have been swamped by, and in some cases dominated by, this incredibly petty self-conscious version of what it is to be male. It involves a whole lot of dick-swinging and woman-hating and other examples of the most pathetic stuff you've ever seen or heard. It would all be hilarious if it wasn't manifesting in some truly horrible ways. The harassment women have to put up with as a result of some of these self-conscious men is abhorrent. This has sometimes resulted in women who dare to be involved with certain industries, like video games, being threatened, terrorized, and driven from their homes by man-children with plenty of free time and just enough crazy to maybe follow through with their threats.

It's repulsive and sad, and it's so common, in large ways and small. Most men are not terrorists and wouldn't ever threaten a woman. But at some point in a lot of these bro out conversations, some shocking little bit of misogyny will pop up out of nowhere, negatively tinting the entire chat. It's like speaking to an otherwise intelligent person who starts using the word 'gay' as a pejorative, or starts rambling about how we all know people of a certain race are sneaky. I just think, "Really? Is this really something you cling to in an age where we are so well-connected that you can read the words of these people you look down on and hear their innermost thoughts? You define yourself by, and feel stronger for stomping on this other group, a group of people who are participating just as integrally as you, if not more so, in building the future? You're making your stand about such a silly, backwards, intentionally ignorant ideology as sexism, racism, homophobia, or insert-other-1950s-era-version-of-ignorant-hate-here?"

Mostly it's just the sports thing, guys talking about sports. I'm not interested in sports, and it's a bummer when someone who, themselves not terribly interested in sports, brings up the subject because of this guy-to-guy reflex.

But I know that part of me is on guard at all times around other guys, even the ones who seem more interested in talking sports, because of that potential dive into something really loathsome. The chance that someone I was beginning to like will fly a different flag once we've moved past the "I'm maybe threatened by you so let's talk about women's parts first" stage of the conversation. It's just so disappointing, on an individual level, but also for the gender.

I know that this is not a new problem. Even the concept of chivalry, which so many people gaze at longingly and recall fondly, was predicated on keeping women from having any power within society. It manifested in a different way than outright violence, certainly, but a prison is a prison, whether it's built of flowers and tassels or steel and stone.

Today, though, we have so many capabilities we've never had before. I can sit here, in this bar, and connect with anyone on the planet. Many people despair at the direction society is going, as we spend an increasing amount of time buried in our devices and ignoring the people around us. But I don't think this is all bad. There are certainly things in our immediate environments that warrant our attention, but what the decriers of modern technology fail to realize is that perhaps the people on the other ends of those Twitter streams or text message conversations are simply far more interesting, or far better conversationalists than the people at the bar, sitting within speaking range.

Since the dawn of agriculture and modern humankind, we've only ever had access to the people, ideas, and resources we could see and touch in the immediacy of our environment. Today, we have access to people, things, and concepts from all over the world, even beyond the world, transmitted down from orbit and from deep space.

Is it any wonder, then, that we might ignore the pithy, the annoying, the familiar, the predictable, in favor of something new? Reach out to connect with someone who's a better intellectual match rather than just a geographic one?

In dating, in doing business, in making friends and swapping stories, isn't our time better spent connecting with those who are solid matches, rather than the chance occupants of the seat next to us at the bar?

I'm a big fan of serendipity, of indulging in what the world offers me, unplanned and unscripted. I like meeting new people, seeing new things, and usually these people and things are tangible, right there next to me. This is why I travel: to be exposed to ideas that are unfamiliar to me.

That said, much of what launches us out into the world, gives us the excuse to extract ourselves from the lives we were handed as children, is the possibility of something better, whatever that word may mean for the individual in question.

Technology has given us immensely powerful mechanisms

of discovering a type of 'better' that couldn't have been conceived of by people even a generation earlier, and the upset this is causing is understandable, but also unstoppable. It provides us with the opportunity to explore new options and consider new possibilities. It's giving us the chance to learn from each other, to explore ideas that never would have come to us otherwise due to our positions in the world, the cultural spaces we occupy, or the ingrained perspectives from which we view things.

We have access to amplified versions of what came before, both the good and the bad. More harassment and bullying, more threats and tools that enable violence, but the opposite as well. The majority of what happens on these networks are net positives for the world and for the global conversation. We're fortunate to take part, all of us who have access to it, who are able to be nodes in the human omni-brain that is the internet. Even if we're not making full use of it yet, at least we're aware of each other. At least we're aware of a world beyond the bar, beyond the beach, beyond the oft-ogled bodies of passersby, beyond the salespeople and the boats and the sports talk.

This era of increased communication and awareness is not a genie that can be put back into its bottle, and it's best that we figure out how to imagine and phrase our desires correctly, because what we're exposed to and the power to which we have access will only increase in intensity from this point forward. We'll want to make sure we wish for the right things, while also learning to live with the consequences of other people's wishes.

CONFIDENCE

I'm staring at toes. Five of them. They're perhaps four feet from my face, poking through the front end of a flip flop. They belong to a man.

I can't stop staring because 1. I'm lying face-down on a table, my head held steady in a padded hole cut in its surface, allowing me to breathe while my muscles are being attacked, pulled, prodded, warmed up, tensed and slackened, and occasionally karate chopped with a loose, non-weaponized hand, and the foot is right there in my line of sight, and 2. because the toenails are immaculate, trimmed just so, the proportion of nail-to-toe mathematically precise, like tiny pyramids, their faces no doubt calculated to the sum of pi to seven or eight decimal places. The nails are also coated with a clear glaze that looks authoritative rather than feminine. My toenails have never, and likely will never, look so good.

The man attached to the toenails is missing part of his left arm: his hand, wrist, and the end-portion of his forearm were taken at the same time as his eyes, sight and partial dexterity simultaneously lost in a dynamite fishing accident years before. He became a certified massage therapist after the accident, learning, as many blind persons do, to utilize the senses they have left to the fullest possible extent. I didn't realize he was missing one of his hands until I was flipped over onto my back and had a full-body view of the man working on me. He's so good at his craft that most of the details just fade into the background, lost in a general 'oh, that's nice' vibe.

I almost didn't find this man and his massage table. I love massages, but the caliber of salesmanship in Boracay leaves something to be desired. My entire body tenses up in preparation for the audible onslaught of salespeople any time I leave my apartment, and those offering massages are some of the worst. They scream the same keywords over and over, step in front of you as you walk, scrambling to force little advertisements into your hands, the same as those divvied out by the hawkers in the next tent over, and the next, and the next, not a one of them standing out in any way except perhaps in the intensity of their self-promotional shamelessness and ability to squeeze promises out of passersby, not stepping out of their way until they concede that, yes, fine maybe they'll have a massage tomorrow. The prices on all their signs, these signs also carbon copies of one another, drop precipitously throughout the week, and each group competes with the other to pull in the most clients.

The one-armed man doesn't lower his prices. He doesn't shout, doesn't harass, doesn't desperately scramble to guilt or trick patrons into lying on his table. I've walked by him every day, and now, coming to the end of my time here on the island, I decided to get a massage, but realized that I didn't want to give any money to those people who had so completely ruined much of my experience of the island with their always-on Vegas-scale broadcasting. I asked for recommendations from a few people I trusted, and they all told me about the same guy. This dude is legit, they told me. Twice the cost of anyone else, but worth it.

Sold.

It turned out that his table was only a few minutes walk from my apartment. I never noticed him before because he's set back from the path and waits calmly on the sand, his table and chair sheltered from the sun by a tarp, his tiny business shingle dwarfed by the neon colors and enormous fonts of every other sign in the area. For a day or two after hearing about him I glanced his way each time I passed by. He was seldom without a client, despite his calm, quiet demeanor. I finally approached him one afternoon just after lunch, asked if he was available, and settled onto the table when he smiled and welcomed me.

There's a confidence in being able to present oneself without extreme advertising efforts or marketing gimmickry. Nearly the whole population of this island seems to think that by shouting louder, approaching more aggressively, dropping their prices more wantonly, they'll pull in more business, will make more money, will fill their coffers. These are short-term efforts with long-term negative consequences, and the same sales ideology has turned the internet into a showroom of pathetic me-too products and valueless brands. Such frantic, conviction-less efforts create a race to the bottom, in both price and value. I'll gladly pay twice as much to a man who not only doesn't bedevil me on the daily, but who takes pride in his work, and is willing to charge an honest fee for the value he provides.

There are two restaurants that stand out from all the others in my neighborhood. Even tucked amidst the Thai food, Indian food, Italian food, Swedish food, German food, American (cowboy-style!) food, and a fair few Filipino food offerings — with their external facades all approximating the same 'we're on the beach, so chill out' attitude, paint chipped, metal roofs rusted, bundles of electrical cable tangling across floors and at eyebrow-height across doorways — the signs for this pair of establishments stand out.

Both display color spectrums otherwise unseen in this place, the first a primary blue that leans toward turquoise, the other a primary yellow, dazzling in its intensity. Both make use of these main colors fearlessly, slathering their shops and signs and even their workers in paint and shirts that reflect their hue-based branding. The blue shop, a burger place, has a white-and-red Italian-restaurant-tablecloth pattern, flipped so the squares become diamonds, as its supplementary graphic, while the yellow shop, a breakfast and high-end diner food joint, has stark white brick walls and matte black ornamentation to reinforce its visually contrasty presence.

These two restaurants stood out to me immediately in part because they were so familiar. I'd never seen them before, of course, but I felt like I had. Neither would be at all out of place in Portland or Seattle, or anywhere across the United States where so-called 'hipster food' is being served to the hungry masses.

Their menus, likewise, played to my expectations. Fewer options than most other restaurants in the area, each one with a flowery description of the simple, homemade, handcrafted, locally sourced cuisine offered up for your enjoyment. Every dish served is gorgeous, artfully arranged, Instagrammable.

That these two establishments are somewhat predictable is heartening to me. They represent a movement in the food industry that promotes higher quality at a slightly higher price, rather than a low-end, low-grade experience, predicated on the fast food model of yesteryear. Instead of aiming low and hitting the mark square in the unimpressive center, shops like this aim for a very respectable above average and typically deliver more than that.

It's not French Laundry, you're not going to have life-changing food at these places, but you're also not going to pay hundreds of dollars for it. They've simplified and focused, have decided what they want to do well and what they can safely leave on the cutting room floor. They deliver a purified version of what we've had before, and offer a clear point of view that's expressed loud and clear, even in a competitive restaurant ecosystem like this island.

Particularly in a loud environment, those who speak with calm confidence are heard most clearly. These are the people and businesses who inspire us, prod us forward, make us smile with surprise and tell our friends about what evoked that smile. In the age of sharing, the age of selfies, the age of emergent personal brands that coalesce without us even trying, we're each of us trying to associate ourselves with things, brands, and other people who help us self-define. The logo on this bag tells part of my story because the company is represents stands for this specific set of ideals. The food on my plate does the same, and the music I'm listening to adds further details to the story of me.

There's a shift occurring in the world of business that incentivizes us to be honest, and to be true to who we are and what we believe. Those who are doing well, who are growing or choosing not to grow despite having the opportunity, are the individuals and brands that have taken the time to know themselves. Who have clearly expressed their origin stories and catalysts, their motive forces and reward systems. We choose who and what to associate ourselves with based on the stories they tell, and now more than ever a story that rings false will be exposed as such, but a story that is true, and one that resonates, one that is shared in a way that allows it to be told and retold, to be appropriated by others and used as a shortcut definition for who they are and what they believe, these are the stories that last. These are the stories we're all telling.

As the massage therapist begins to work on my feet and calves, I turn my head and watch the beach-cleaners work. They rake the sand in starburst patterns, scraping away debris, sticks, palm fronds, coconut shells. The beach itself is purified by their actions, the landscape itself changing shape and attitude, becoming the refined idea of a beach rather than a real, true to life version of the same. Like the toenails I was staring at until a moment before, the shore is slowly carved into the proper shape, coated with something preservative to ensure it shines in just the right way.

It would be silly to rage against this, to demand the version of the beach I enjoyed during the recent typhoon, a debris-mottled landscape in which the locals hunker down amongst the palm trees, alternatingly playing in the water and hiding from the wind, smiling their happiness about being out to play while most of the tourists stay inside, tending to emotional wounds inflicted by the weather that was ruining their vacation plans.

We all have different ideals. We all have different concepts of what great service is, what makes for good food, what well-tended toenails and beaches look like.

There are positives to even the worst performers in the food service landscape. The corporations that are at least partially responsible for the deterioration of physical health and wellness in the United States also helped develop many of the technologies that are allowing this new, 'hipster food' revolution to occur. They innovated the hell out of production, distribution, and management systems. They invented new machines, new organizational structures, new marketing models, and all of these things are being appropriated and riffed on by the barbarians at the gate.

We're always, all of us, cultivating and turning the soil where those who replace us will grow. It seems like a tragedy each time, because a structure we've come to respect, to expect, to base our plans upon, must shatter for the fresh-born sprouts to stand a chance.

This type of change is difficult to live through, certainly, but it's integral to growth and development; to evolution. It's important to remember that Rome had to be destroyed for Europe to be born. No matter how much we might claim to desire continuity, the only thing that ever brings true, positive change, is the destruction of the last best thing of which we could conceive. We have to make room so that new, amazing things can start growing.

SIGNIFICANCE

The beach is nearly gone today, the tide flooding inward to claim the sand it deposited days or years before, the water tickling the toes of the bare few tourists who brave the still-unsteady weather that is warmer than in the days of the typhoon, but still hazy, still dark, will still require some filters if any photos taken are going to impress friends back home.

It's my last day here in Boracay, and my mind conspires to bring significance to this fact. It notes that the ocean is somehow beckoning to me, waving (ha!) goodbye, hoping that I remember it fondly as I pack my belongings and board the assortment of vehicles that will return me to the country from whence I came.

It seemed that fewer salespeople shouted at me today, fewer hawkers of cheap wares stepped into my path and obstructed my view. It may be that they aren't optimistic about their business potential in weather like this. Today is a moment between extremes during which wind could stir back up and chase the tourists toward the shelters of their polished resort rooms and gated inland pools, or the sun could creep out, drying the many surfaces, the roofs and tents and tricycles, that have been sopping wet for days, forcing even the most diehard of beach bum to pull on a shirt and scowl at the ineffectiveness of their flip flops.

My mind scrambles to make connections like this on days that are perceived to be unlike other days. My last day in Mayoyao was the same: it seemed as if the weather was just so, the people were just so, the day was different from all other days I spent there. Here on the beach this feeling is even more extreme because I don't have friends, well-known quantities, to use as absolute metrics for these changes. I can't use their responses and reactions to guide my own, to see if it's the world around me that has changed, or merely my interpretation of that world.

If you're not careful, leaving a place can seem a bit like the Archilles and the Tortoise portion of Zeno's Paradox. This is a thought experiment in which a race is run, and the distance between the runners and the finish line are reduced by half, and then half, and then half again, forever. The finish line is never reached because each increment of time feels longer, stretched out, due to the perceived significance of the moment. It takes no time at all for most of the month to fly by, but the final day takes just as long as that month, and the final hour as long as that day. The final minutes before you leave a place take the longest as physics seem to cease operating entirely, and the moment, the anticipation, the goodbyes and last-minute photographs to remember this place better, the doubts and regrets and everything else, it adds up. It becomes a mental burden in a way. A lump of memories that are largely meaningless, at least when compared to the other moments, the days in which we imbued less significance. The times when nothing much happened at all, but the sunset was beautiful, the weather was perfect. Nothing to write home about, but moments worth experiencing. Worth remembering, if you can make yourself remember.

The deck is stacked against us in this regard, though. We're programmed to notice milestones, and there are few lifestyle adjustments more noteworthy than a move to new geography. A change in location represents a change in a person, and this is both perceptual and literal, because moving is a milestone that gives us psychological permission to change, grow, adjust, adopt new lessons we may have learned but haven't yet implemented. Surrounding ourselves with a new crowd, new weather, wearing new clothes, all of these things allow us to be whomever we want, to build a new sense of self, reinforced by the people around us. We no longer have anyone consciously or subconsciously holding us to an established set of habits, routines, mannerisms, or opinions.

We don't have physical reminders of these things, either: the bar on the corner, the street vendor with whom we exchange hellos, the restaurant that serves that dish that you tell yourself you need to stop eating so that you can try something else on the menu, but which you can't stop eating, it's too good. These things become part of us, part of our day, part of our lifestyle, part of who we are because we are defined by how we interact with the physical world around us.

We are all heroes of our own stories, and the way we write these stories, the way we see ourselves as a part of the narratives that play out around us, is informed by the media we take in our entire lives. In books, movies, plays, video games, there are protagonists we come to know, come to recognize and root for. We may come to see something of ourselves in these people, or find them so appallingly unknowable that their very foreignness compels us to pay attention, to not look away, to learn and seek clarity and relevance.

At the end of a story we find morality, though not always tied up neatly in a bow as with the traditional tales, the Aesop's Fables and holy books and other such collections of oral tradition, the tales passed on from generation to generation, filling the void that textbooks and multiple choice tests and instructions from parents would eventually come to occupy. Most good stories present their lessons with a certain moral ambiguity. The person reading or watching or otherwise consuming the tale is able to choose, if not their own adventure, certainly their own interpretation of the events contained with it. Anything more concrete is considered to be heavy-handed and obvious, not subjective enough for modern audiences who recognize that there is more than one way to view any event, for people who grew up in a world full of flawed heroes and sympathetic villains. Full of corrupt leaders and terrorists who are also freedom fighters, depending on your point of view, culture of origin, and political leanings.

The complexity of these stories is what prepares us for the real world, prepares us to live out our own stories, to be the heroes of our own narratives, and to perhaps share something of what we've learned with the world. To tie it up neatly with a bow, or maybe just attempt to share it in a way that doesn't make the story lame.

But there are no clean narratives, not in real life, just as there's no inherent significance in the stories that play out around us.

We imbue our actions and the randomness of the world around us with meaning. This is a power we have. We choose to see opportunities as such, we choose to see luck as something beyond coincidence, and ignore that our luck is often the opposite for someone else. We choose to take away lessons from some moments, and to leave other lessons, often those that are seemingly in opposition to what we want to learn, on the table.

This is a good thing. This means that we can make of any moment whatever we like. We aren't limited to finding significance on certain days or in rare moments. We can look out at the ocean and think, "This is an important moment I want to remember. The colors of the water, the sound of the children playing, the taste of the air. This is meaningful to me because it represents something I enjoy, something that makes me happy." We can do this. We can choose our own significance and how we want to see the world and live our lives.

Other significance is handed to us because of how the larger bulk of society sees things. Holidays and weekends, astronomical events like days and nights, months and years. We flip out over Y2Ks and decades and millennia, failing to recognize that time is something we invented, a shared unit of measurement that we agreed upon as a species. The universe, creatures, and other things that are not human and have therefore not made such an agreement couldn't care less that it's New Years Eve, and won't hold back their lessons until you're paying attention on such a day, at such a moment.

We choose which of our stories are important, which of our days we remember, which of our relationships last and what impact all of these things have on our lives. We are the oracles of our own destinies, the writers of our own plays, the fortune tellers reading our own palms, being told and telling ourselves exactly what we want to, and perhaps need to, hear.

There's significance in everything that we do, even if it's not the significance we're brought up to believe is there. It's valuable and should be treasured. And our stories, whether or not they come with a neat and clear moral at the end, are worth telling.

AFTER

TURBULENCE

It's my second flight of the day. The first took me from Manila to Tokyo, and after a few hours layover, I'm in the air again, tucked cozily into a pile composed of blanket, a tiny complimentary pillow, a seat belt, and headphone wires. I'm secure and settled, ready for an extended trip across the Pacific, back to Los Angeles. The starting point for a new round of adventures.

The first jolt is shocking for its brevity and calm-shattering emergence. But it's not too bad. Just a sudden moment of disarray about an hour into an otherwise uneventful flight. These things happen. You learn to cope, to glance at the flight attendants to see if there's actually anything to worry about, to be reassured by their calm, reliable boredom.

The next movement is different. More of a lurch. The plane doesn't bounce or stutter, it shifts in space, as if some titanic hand has grabbed the tail of the craft and scooted it around a little, first to the left, then to the right, then straight down, then a little more to the side, and continues on like that for few seconds. When the plane in which you're flying, which itself is over a vast expanse of ocean, starts to be rearranged in space, no matter how many seconds actually pass it feels like epochs have transpired. Eons.

The flight attendants exchange neutral glances as they hurry about the cabin, making sure everyone has their seat belts on, pointing out the now-lit sign indicating that we need to buckle up. They're moving calmly, and their calm transfers to me.

All is well. I lean back further into the seat.

Then comes a frantic tilt and realignment, the front of the plane pivoting first one way then another, my seat bouncing me up and down, at times hurling me airborne, that feeling of vertigo starting in my stomach and slamming up into my throat. There's a crowd of Japanese school children sitting behind and in front of me, young teenagers I think, who shriek wildly, their high-pitched hubbub adding to the groan of the plane's joints, the visible wobble of the wings, and the ongoing shuttering of the overhead compartments.

The attendants' eyes are wide, now. Their faces are still calm, their voices reassuring when speaking to ticket-holders, but when speaking into the phone with the pilot and exchanging instructions between themselves, there's a sliver of panic in their voices.

The whole plane goes into lockdown. The attendants rush through the cabin to check the seat belts one more time, then clamp themselves down as soon as they reach the end of the aisle. The lights are flickering, and are eventually turned off. It's barely bright enough to see, but the flickering was causing anxiety, while the darkness calms, cloaking the worse of the worry-lines showing on faces throughout the plane.

I tap the screen embedded on the seat in front of me, pulling up an auto-updated register of the flight's information. Over the course of the next three hours, we go from 32,000 feet to 33,000, then up to 34, 35. Our speed fluctuates wildly, sometimes hustling us toward the West Coast of the US faster than seems feasible, sometimes almost holding still, carried only by the wind and the prayers of some of the more religious and religious-in-a-foxhole members of the plane's population.

This isn't the worst turbulence I've been in, but it's the longest-lasting. The plane shutters and shakes, to lesser and greater degrees, for the entirety of the trip. When the plane comes in for a landing, I release a deep breath I hadn't realized I was holding. Clumps of passengers break out into a round of applause. We're all happy to have made it through such a thing. We all have one more story to share with our friends and family, with blog readers and book browsers.

We made it. We were put in a difficult position and we came out the other side, unscathed and unscarred. All future flights will be easy in comparison. All future trips will be more difficult to justify, as the memory of what can happen while in transit is recalled, coloring our choices, helping us choose the paths we walk.

Turbulence helps us appreciate the calm, collected, in-control moments with greater intensity. It outlines the joy, helps us remember the happiness, makes us more likely to pursue fun, and whittles away some of the concerns we have, some of the hesitations and limitations between us and living as fully as we possibly can. Staring death in the eye makes you take life more seriously. Getting a taste of what danger might look like, how it might feel, how you might respond to it, hoists that consideration to the top of your priority pole and gives you the chance to amble unswervingly onward or hasten into a head-bowed retreat.

Instability reminds us to stabilize. Danger reminds us to buckle up.

A life lacking external variables and potential perils is a life without clarity. It's a calm walk down a smooth path, free of challenges and concerns, but also lacking in growth and perspective.

Motion, to me, is an exercise in balance and persistence. You shift your weight, adjust your stance, and reach out with your senses to understand where you are in space, all so that you can stay on your feet. So that you can sync up with the world as it moves rather than being knocked flat by it.

But you have to stick with it and improve your equilibrium over time. Frayed and rattled as each new experience might leave you, persistence allows you to become your own turbulence, your own force of nature, capable of shaking things up and moving people just by being who you are and doing what you exist to do.

ABOUT THE AUTHOR

Colin Wright is an author, entrepreneur, and full-time traveler. He was born in 1985 and lives in a new country every four months; the country is voted on by his readers. More info at colin.io.

CONNECT WITH COLIN ONLINE

Blog
Exilelifestyle.com

Work
Colin.io

Twitter
Twitter.com/colinismyname

Facebook
Facebook.com/colinwright

Instagram
Instagram.com/colinismyname

Tumblr
Colinismyname.tumblr.com

ALSO BY COLIN WRIGHT

Nonfiction

Some Thoughts About Relationships
Considerations
Curation is Creation
Act Accordingly
Start a Freedom Business
How to Travel Full-Time
Networking Fundamentals
How to Be Remarkable
Personal Branding

Memoirs

Come Back Frayed
Iceland India Interstate
My Exile Lifestyle

Fiction Series

A Tale of More
Real Powers

Novels

Hollow Words Rich With Meaning
Puncture Up
Ordovician

Short Fiction Collections

Coffee with the Other Man
So This Is How I Go
Mean Universe
7 or 8 Ways to End the World
7 or 8 More Ways to End the World